INTRODUCTION TO
Legal and Ethical Issues in Sport

First Edition

Marissa W. Pollick, J.D.

cognella®
SAN DIEGO

Bassim Hamadeh, CEO and Publisher
Jennifer Codner, Senior Field Acquisitions Editor
Anne Jones, Project Editor
Susana Christie, Senior Developmental Editor
Abbey Hastings, Production Editor
Asfa Arshi, Graphic Design Assistant
Trey Soto, Licensing Specialist
Natalie Piccotti, Director of Marketing
Kassie Graves, Senior Vice President, Editorial
Jamie Giganti, Director of Academic Publishing

Copyright © 2023 by Cognella, Inc. All rights reserved. No part of this publication may be reprinted, reproduced, transmitted, or utilized in any form or by any electronic, mechanical, or other means, now known or hereafter invented, including photocopying, microfilming, and recording, or in any information retrieval system without the written permission of Cognella, Inc. For inquiries regarding permissions, translations, foreign rights, audio rights, and any other forms of reproduction, please contact the Cognella Licensing Department at rights@cognella.com.

Trademark Notice: Product or corporate names may be trademarks or registered trademarks and are used only for identification and explanation without intent to infringe.

Cover image: Copyright © 2009 iStockphoto LP/procurator.
Copyright © 2015 iStockphoto LP/LemonTreeImages.

Printed in the United States of America.

cognella ACADEMIC PUBLISHING
3970 Sorrento Valley Blvd., Ste. 500, San Diego, CA 92121

BRIEF CONTENTS

Acknowledgments   xi
Introduction   xiii

    Chapter 1.   Law and Ethics for Sport Managers   1

    Chapter 2.   Sport-Related Injuries and Managing Health and Safety   15

    Chapter 3.   Contract Law and Sport   33

    Chapter 4.   Title IX and Sex Discrimination in Sport   63

    Chapter 5.   Employment Law and Diversity in Sport Organizations   85

    Chapter 6.   Criminal Law: Sport Violence and Athlete Misconduct   107

References   125
About the Author   131

DETAILED CONTENTS

Acknowledgments   xi
Introduction   xiii

Chapter 1. Law and Ethics for Sport Managers   1

Opening Statement   1
I. The Law   2
Fundamentals of the U.S. Legal System   2
- Overview   2
- Civil Law Versus Criminal Law   2
- Sources of Law   3
- State and Federal Court Systems   3
- Civil Lawsuit—Typical Proceedings   4
- Glossary of Laws and Legal Terminology   8

II. The Ethics   10
Ethical Concepts for Sport Managers and Participants   10
- Overview   10
- Ethics in Sport Competition   11
  - Youth Sports   11
  - Intercollegiate Sports   12
  - Professional Sports   12
- Ethics in Sport Business   12
- Glossary of Ethical Concepts and Terminology   13

Closing Arguments   14
Study Questions   14

Chapter 2. Sport-Related Injuries and Managing Health and Safety   15

Opening Statement   15
I. The Law   16
Tort Law: Fundamentals   16
- Overview   16
- Negligence   16
  - Duty (Standard of Care)   17
  - Breach of Duty   17
  - Causation   17
  - Damages   18

  Vicarious Liability   19
  Defenses to Negligence   20
   Assumption of Risk   21
    Comparative Negligence   22
  Gross Negligence   22
  Product Liability   23
   Negligence Theory   23
   Breach of Warranty Theory   23
   Strict Liability Theory   24
  Intentional Torts   24
   Assault   25
   Battery   25
 Managing Risk   25
 Setting a Precedent   26
 II. The Ethics   26
  Case Scenarios   26
 Closing Arguments   30
 Study Questions   31

Chapter 3.   Contract Law and Sport   33

 Opening Statement   33
 I. The Law   34
 Contract Law: Fundamentals   34
  Overview   34
  Elements   34
   Offer   35
   Acceptance   35
   Consideration   35
   Legality   35
   Capacity   36
  Contract Interpretation and Breach   36
   Contract Interpretation   36
   Breach of Contract   36
  Remedies and Damages for Breach   36
   Compensatory Damages   37
   Consequential Damages   37
   Liquidated Damages   37
   Specific Performance   38
  Contract Administration: Best Practices for Management   38
 Sample Sport Contracts and Key Provisions   38
   Collective Bargaining Agreements   39
   Game Contract   39

  Facility Lease Agreements 41
  Endorsement Contracts 41
  Agent Representation 42
  National Letter of Intent and Scholarships 43
  NIL Agreements 44
  Participation Waivers and Releases 44
Coaching Contracts 47
 Material Terms in Coaching Contracts 50
  Term 50
  Salary 50
  Bonuses 51
  Termination 53
 Additional Terms 54
  Duties 54
  Perquisites 54
  Reassignment 55
  Mitigation 55
 Future Trends in Coaching Contracts 56
Setting a Precedent 57
II. The Ethics 57
 Case Scenarios 57
Closing Arguments 61
Study Questions 61

Chapter 4. Title IX and Sex Discrimination in Sport 63

Opening Statement 63
I. The Law 64
Title IX 64
 Legislative History 65
 Early Cases and Policy Developments 65
 Athletic Compliance Regulations 68
  Participation 68
  Scholarships 69
  Treatment 69
 Overall Impact and Misconceptions 70
 Key Legal Developments and OCR Guidance 73
 NIL and Title IX 74
 Sexual Harassment and Sexual Assault 74
 Sexual Harassment and Sexual Assault Case Examples 75
 NCAA Role and Authority 76
Setting a Precedent 77

II. The Ethics   77
   Case Scenarios   77
Closing Arguments   83
Study Questions   83

Chapter 5. Employment Law and Diversity in Sport Organizations   85

Opening Statement   85
I. The Law   86
Employment Law: Fundamentals   86
   Employment at Will Doctrine   86
   Equal Pay Act of 1963 (EPA)   86
      Legislative History   87
      Relationship to Title VII and the Ledbetter Act   87
      EPA—Elements and Defenses   88
      The EPA as Applied to Female Coaches and Athletes   88
   Title VII of the Civil Rights Act of 1964 (Title VII)   90
      Legislative History   90
      Unlawful Employment Practices Under Title VII   91
      Applicability of Title VII to Sport   92
   Age Discrimination in Employment Act (ADEA)   97
   Americans with Disabilities Act (ADA)   97
      Applicability of ADA to Sport   98
   College Athletes as Employees   99
      Worker's Compensation Law   99
      Minimum Wage and Overtime Pay   99
      Ability to Organize as a Union   100
Setting a Precedent   101
II. The Ethics   101
   Case Scenarios   101
Closing Arguments   105
Study Questions   105

Chapter 6. Criminal Law: Sport Violence and Athlete Misconduct   107

Opening Statement   107
I. The Law   108
Criminal Law: Fundamentals   108
   Overview   108
   Criminal Assault and Battery   109
      Assault   110
      Battery   110
   Extreme Sport Violence—Case Examples   110
      Hockey   110

   Football 112
   Baseball 112
   Basketball 113
  Violence to Gain a Competitive Advantage 114
  Punishment: League Handling Versus Governmental Intervention 115
  Off the Field Criminal Conduct 116
Setting a Precedent 118
II. The Ethics 118
  Case Scenarios 118
Closing Arguments 122
Study Questions 123

References 125
About the Author 131

ACKNOWLEDGMENTS

This book came about when my academic unit asked that I revamp my undergraduate sports law curriculum into a new course, entitled Legal and Ethical Issues in Sport. This was a welcome request that I wholeheartedly supported for many years. The interrelationship between law and ethics is both fascinating and important for sport managers and the sport industry at large. In fact, my sports law class lectures often included discussions of business ethics that applied to the assigned legal cases. Yet, I was unable to find an academic textbook that specifically matched the curriculum I envisioned for my new course. Sports law textbooks were very good but insufficient to fully examine ethical issues in sport. My collection of ethics resources was equally valuable; however, it lacked a synthesis with the fundamentals of law and legal cases. After discussing my proposal with Cognella Academic Publishing, I was excited to undertake this project as author of my own academic textbook, *Introduction to Legal and Ethical Issues in Sport*.

First, thank you to the outstanding staff at Cognella, who guided me at all steps of the book and this First Edition. Specifically, I am grateful for the assistance of Senior Field Acquisitions Editor Jennifer Codner, Project Editor Anne Jones, Senior Project Editor Michelle Piehl, Senior Developmental Editor Susana Christie, and Production Editor Abbey Hastings. Each was enthusiastic, patient, and supportive of my work throughout the process.

Next, I want to thank my students and colleagues at the University of Michigan. I have served on the sport management faculty at the graduate and undergraduate levels since 2004. Teaching is tremendously rewarding and has been a perfect transition from my long career as an attorney and civil litigator in cases involving commercial contracts, employment discrimination, and Title IX. Many of my former students expressed appreciation for my classes and professional experience and are now pursuing their own successful careers in law and sport. Two of my former UM students contributed research that I relied on in this book. Jenna Flory did excellent work in researching and summarizing several tort cases that are discussed in Chapter 2. In Chapter 6, I included an ethics case scenario on state-sponsored doping based on work by my former graduate student and graduate assistant Rob Sroka. I have benefited from my UM colleagues and their enormous breadth of knowledge and experience in sport business. I am also grateful to former Associate Dean for Faculty and Undergraduate Affairs Tom Templin, who enthusiastically supported my teaching and writing.

This book was significantly enhanced by the work of two contributing authors: Dana Drew Shaw, JD, and Mechelle Zarou, Esq. Over the years, I worked with many distinguished attorneys as colleagues and advocates. Dana and Mechelle are among the best. Dana has represented college coaches in contract negotiations and contributed to the Coaching Contracts section of Chapter 3. Mechelle is a highly regarded labor and employment lawyer and contributed to the sections on the Equal Pay Act, Title VII, and related case analyses in Chapter 5.

It is my honor to teach law and ethics at my alma mater. My book draws on my some of my personal experiences at the University of Michigan, as an undergraduate history major, student-athlete, and law student at the University of Michigan Law School. For some of my students, this book will reveal to them for the first time a history of discrimination at their own school, including the university's early opposition and resistance to Title IX, and the underrepresentation and disparate treatment of women in our educational programs, including athletics. However, this is a story I believe must be told and from which many lessons may be learned, including the fact that leaders do not necessarily do the right thing for the right reasons.

Finally, thank you to my wonderful family and friends for supporting my writing and advocacy. My special gratitude goes to Elizabeth Ritt for her encouragement and insight from decades of experience in college coaching and athletic administration. This book is dedicated to my parents who inspired my passion for law, teaching, and social justice.

INTRODUCTION

As a general principle, we expect sport managers to follow the law and behave in an ethical manner. However, the history of sport tells us that such expectations are increasingly unrealistic. The abundance of case law, legal disputes, and ethics scandals in sport reflects conduct that frequently violates norms, rules, laws, and moral standards of right and wrong. It is essential to confront legal and ethical issues in the sport industry in an understandable way for sport management students who are unfamiliar with the complexities and requirements of the law and business ethics. This begins with the basic notion that law and ethics are distinct. Conduct might be legal but unethical, and therefore, improper. Policies and procedures must be implemented to ensure compliance with laws and regulations in sport settings to prevent harm to others and reduce legal liability to the sport organization. Adherence to the highest ethical standards is also necessary to maintain integrity of sport competition and the sport industry at large.

This textbook examines the fundamentals of key areas of law that impact the sport industry and related ethical concepts that guide behavior and decision-making in sport settings. Each chapter is structured in a comparable way to distinguish applicable legal and ethical issues in a particular subject area. Each chapter begins with an Opening Statement that contains an overview of the specific areas of law and ethics. That is followed by Learning Objectives, for students to understand what is expected from the respective chapter content. Each chapter is then divided into two major sections: I (The Law) and II (The Ethics). Section I sets forth fundamentals of the relevant area of law and case examples in sport. It also includes a list of key cases under the heading Setting a Precedent. Section II contains Case Scenarios, which present and analyze ethical dilemmas (real and hypothetical) that arise in sport and the sport industry. Sections I and II are followed by a Closing Argument, which summarizes the main points and concepts of the chapter. In several chapters, there are Case Notes in text boxes to identify and discuss an important case decision in that area of law. Full case citations, statutory citations, as well as other sources and authorities for each chapter, are found in References at the end of the book.

Chapter 1 provides an overview of the U.S. legal system, including the distinction between civil law and criminal law, the sources of U.S. law, and how civil lawsuits proceed under our state and federal court systems. Section I also includes a glossary of key laws, legal terms, and phrases that are examined and referenced throughout this text. Chapter 1 also addresses basic ethical concepts that apply to sport competition and the sport industry. It begins with consideration of the "win at all costs" mentality that leads to cheating in competitive sports in general. It then examines the specific areas where ethical decision-making is central to the business of sport. Section II also includes a glossary of key terms and phrases related to ethical principles that arise in case scenarios throughout this text.

Chapter 2 examines sport-related injuries and how to manage health and safety in sport organizations. Section I addresses the fundamental legal principles of tort law, the elements of a legal claim for negligence, and typical sport scenarios that give rise to negligence claims. In addition, it examines other tort claims that occur on and off the field in sport, including gross negligence, product liability, and intentional torts such as battery and assault. Legal defenses to negligence in sport settings are addressed, with particular attention given to the doctrine of assumption of risk. Many case examples are provided throughout Section I to illustrate principles of tort law and the process of risk management in sport organizations. Section II of this chapter addresses the ethical aspects of decision-making by schools, coaches, manufacturers, and other sport managers to protect others from health and safety risks and dangers. The Case Scenarios feature various ethical concepts and failures when schools, sport organizations, or manufacturers rely primarily on financial projections and potential legal exposure when developing and implementing their risk management policies, rather than prioritizing health and safety.

Chapter 3 addresses the fundamental legal principles of contract law. It sets forth the required elements of contract formation, as well as the typical sport scenarios that give rise to a legal claim of breach of contract. As a helpful guide for students, this chapter also includes sample contract language found in typical sport contracts, with particular emphasis on coaching contracts at the intercollegiate level, which are the subject of much public interest. An explanation is provided for how sport managers can implement best practices for contract drafting and contract administration within their school or sport organization. This chapter then addresses ethical aspects of certain sport contracts, as well as the NCAA's amateurism model. Ethically, many argue that college athletes are being exploited under this model. There are ethical concerns when student-athletes are limited in their ability to earn money from their own name or likeness, or precluded from being paid for their athletic talents by agents or corporate sponsors. There are also ethical concerns with eligibility rules and the imposition of academic standards as a condition of continued athletic participation in college. This has led to academic fraud scandals at universities with major athletic programs, including the University of North Carolina at Chapel Hill, which is addressed in detail.

Chapter 4 examines sex discrimination in sport. It addresses the legislative history of Title IX and the legal aspects of Title IX as it relates to athletic compliance. In addition, this chapter focuses on how and why Title IX applies to sexual harassment and sexual assault in a school sports context; for example, when alleged perpetrators or victims of sexual misconduct are student-athletes, coaches, or other team personnel. This chapter also analyzes Title IX case law that includes many U.S. Supreme Court cases interpreting the law and its regulations. A number of ethical questions related to sex discrimination in sport are addressed, such as the reasons why many schools have tried to circumvent Title IX regulations, and the ethical issues related to treatment of transgender athletes and sex testing in sport. This chapter also examines major scandals involving cover-ups of sexual assault in college athletic programs and sexual abuse in youth sports.

Chapter 5 addresses the fundamental legal principles of employment law. It explains the doctrine of "employment at will" and legislative exceptions to that doctrine. Various federal civil rights laws, including the Equal Pay Act and Title VII, are discussed in detail, together with relevant case examples in sport. Illegal discrimination in the workplace based on race, color, sex, national origin, religion, age, or disability are examined in detail. This chapter also addresses the ethical aspects of maintaining a nondiscriminatory sport workplace that values principles of diversity, equity, and inclusion. It examines explicit and implicit bias that has permeated sport organizations, often rooted in negative stereotypes, and is reflected in the underrepresentation of women and minorities in coaching and leadership positions.

Chapter 6 addresses the elements of criminal law and potential crimes of assault and battery that occur in sport. These crimes are examined because athletes who participate in inherently dangerous sports, such as boxing, football, and hockey, frequently engage in violent conduct that would be subject to criminal charges if the same acts occurred in a non-sport setting. It explains how criminal matters involve prosecution by the state or federal government, with the possibility of imprisonment, and are subject to a higher burden of proof than civil cases. It looks closely at examples of "on the field" and "on the ice" violence committed by athletes, and factors that should be considered to evaluate appropriate team and league discipline. It also examines the relative merits of league discipline versus governmental intervention in extreme sport violence, particularly when that violence is premeditated or intended to gain a competitive advantage in sport. This chapter also examines criminal and ethical aspects of doping in sport, including state-sponsored doping, which cheats the system and often the athletes themselves. Other forms of cheating in sport are also examined in this context, which do not necessarily involve criminal conduct, but demonstrate that rule breaking and violation of norms are often overlooked or rationalized by a "winning is everything" mentality in sport.

As a final note, as you utilize this textbook, it should provide a firm legal and ethical foundation for sport management students in whatever field they choose to pursue.

Law and Ethics for Sport Managers

CHAPTER 1

Opening Statement

Sport managers must understand fundamental legal and ethical principles that impact sport and the sport industry. From a legal perspective, this includes knowledge of how our U.S. legal system works, as well as key content areas, such as tort law, contract law, employment law, criminal law, and specific laws that prohibit discrimination in schools and the workplace. This knowledge is essential because legal issues consistently arise in sport settings, whether dealing with youth sport, interscholastic sport, intercollegiate sport, professional sport, or other sport-related businesses and organizations. As a sport manager, you also need to recognize legal risks and take appropriate action to minimize them, to protect against harm to employees, fans, spectators, coaches, and athletes, while at the same time reducing the exposure of your sport organization to legal liability. It is not enough, however, for sport managers and organizations to simply refrain from illegal conduct. There are ethical principles that must guide decision-making in sport organizations. This entails refraining from business policies and practices that might be legal yet are ethically or morally wrong. Ethical issues address standards that one should follow based on values and concepts of what is right and wrong. Sport managers consistently face ethical questions in various sport settings related to integrity, fairness, diversity, equity, health and safety, employment practices, financial transparency, and social justice. The same is true for sport participants at all levels who aspire to the values and principles of good sportsmanship and fair play. It is important to recognize that what is deemed legal conduct in a sport setting might still be unethical conduct. The failure to maintain ethical standards is detrimental to sport, sport business, and societal interests, and reflects poorly on individual decision-makers and the organizations they represent.

Section I of this chapter addresses the fundamentals of the U.S. legal system, including the distinction between civil law and criminal law, the sources of U.S. law, and an overview of how civil lawsuits proceed under our state and

LEARNING OBJECTIVES

After reading this chapter, students will:

1. Understand the basic structure of the U.S. legal system
2. Know the differences between civil and criminal law
3. Recognize the vast range of ethical issues facing sport organizations at all levels
4. Understand the definitions of key terms and phrases used in the study of law and ethics

federal court systems. This section also includes a glossary of key laws, legal terms, and phrases that are examined and referenced throughout this text.

Section II of this chapter addresses basic ethical concepts that apply to sport competition and the sport industry. It begins with consideration of the "win at all costs" mentality that leads to cheating in competitive sports in general. It then examines the specific areas where ethical decision-making is central to the business of sport. This section also includes a glossary of key terms and phrases related to ethical principles that arise in case scenarios throughout this text.

I. The Law

Fundamentals of the U.S. Legal System

Overview

Legal issues affect all businesses, including the sport industry. The history and development of sport has been influenced by various federal and state laws, regulations, standards of care, and our U.S. Constitution. Legal disputes are addressed and resolved through our U.S. legal system. This system encompasses different types and areas of law, and provides appropriate forums for parties to present facts and legal arguments to obtain a fair and final determination. Sport managers must be familiar with the U.S. legal system and how litigation (lawsuits between parties) proceeds in that system. They also must recognize the legal rights and responsibilities of sport participants, fans, coaches, administrators, employers, and employees in any sport-related setting, as well as how to manage risk within sport organizations to protect health and safety and reduce organizational liability.

Civil Law Versus Criminal Law

Civil law and criminal law are distinct types of law. Civil law refers to the body of law that relates to private claims between parties, which are enforced by civil lawsuits or causes of action. As is clear in this text, most legal issues relevant to sport management occur in a civil context. Typically, one party sues another in civil court to recover monetary damages for harm caused by the failure of another to act reasonably or comply with legal requirements. Legal topics in this text, such as torts, contracts, employment matters, and sex discrimination in sport, involve civil law and civil lawsuits.

Criminal law involves prosecution by the state or federal government for wrongful acts considered by society to be so egregious that they are a breach of peace. There are state and federal laws that define crimes for a particular jurisdiction, as well as the prescribed punishment, which may include imprisonment. The specific penalties for state crimes, such as assault, battery, or murder, may vary from state to state, and criminal judges sometimes have discretion to impose prison sentences within a certain range of time. Federal crimes include wrongful acts against the federal government, such as tax evasion, bank robbery, or interstate crimes like kidnapping and wire fraud. State crimes are prosecuted by local district attorneys or county prosecutors. Federal crimes are prosecuted by U.S.

attorneys who are appointed by the president to serve as the chief federal law enforcement officer in each federal judicial district.

Sources of Law

One source of U.S. law is "common law," which relates back to the legal system in medieval England. Common law is sometimes referred to as "judge-made" law, or is otherwise known as case law. Cases are legal determinations based on a set of particular facts involving parties with a genuine interest in the controversy (Fine, 1997). The common law system relies on case precedent, as courts develop rules based on prior case decisions involving similar facts and legal issues. This means that lower state courts (trial courts) are bound by decisions of higher (appellate) courts in the same state. In the federal system, the federal district courts are bound by appellate courts within their region (circuit).

Another source of law is federal and state statutes. Statutes are laws that are enacted by legislative bodies at the federal or state level. With cities and municipalities, the laws passed by local governments are generally known as ordinances. Criminal laws are an example of statutory law passed by legislatures at the state and federal levels. Statutory law covers a vast array of legal areas that might apply to sport in various ways. Some examples at the state level include state statutes that regulate sport agents or that mandate concussion safety protocol in schools. At the federal level, examples of federal statutes that impact sport include Title IX, which prohibits sex discrimination in educational programs, and the Amateur Sports Act, which provides the organizational structure and certain trademark protections for the United States Olympic Committee.

Another source of law is known as constitutional law. Constitutional law embodies the rules and regulations that govern the country as well as the rights of the people. The U.S. Constitution sets the legal parameters for what the government can and cannot do, and it outlines the basic rights of its citizens. In addition, every state in the United States has its own constitution by which its citizens are governed. The U.S. Constitution is the supreme law of the land. It was adopted in 1787 and has evolved through the amendment process over the centuries that followed. In 1791, the first U.S. Congress approved ten amendments that guarantee certain individual protections from the power of government. Those amendments are known as the Bill of Rights. Many individual rights and protections under the Bill of Rights apply to states as well.

Another source of law is administrative law. These are rules and regulations passed by administrative agencies, which have authority to regulate certain areas. Examples at the federal level include the Office for Civil Rights, which enforces Title IX and other federal statutes, and the National Labor Relations Board, which oversees federal labor law. There are also many state and local administrative bodies with authority to enact regulations at the state and/or local levels.

State and Federal Court Systems

The U.S. court system comprises different courts at the state and federal levels. There are also, in some cases, specialized courts that only hear certain types of cases, such as tax tribunals or bankruptcy courts. A common misconception about litigation is that cases proceed quickly to conclusion in court through trial. In fact, lawsuits may take years from the time of commencement through pre-trial motions, exchange of documents, witness depositions, trial, and appeal, and most lawsuits are resolved (settled) without trial. In many courts, judges actively engage both sides prior to trial to reach a settlement in lieu of the costly and time-consuming trial process. When a case is voluntarily settled, the court enters an order for dismissal of the civil action and the case is removed from the court trial docket. Settlement agreements between private parties typically include a confidentiality requirement that is binding on both sides.

In the state court system, the lowest court is usually known as the trial court. Trial courts are located in each county throughout the state, and those courts handle lawsuits through trial by judge or jury. In the state system, there is an intermediate level of courts known as appellate courts or state courts of appeal. Appellate courts review the record of the trial court at the request of the losing party and may affirm or reverse the decision, or in some cases send the case back to the trial court for another trial. The highest court in the state system is typically known as the state supreme court, which may hear appeals from the state appellate court.

In the federal court system, the trial courts are known as federal district courts. Each state is divided into a number of federal districts. The state of Michigan, for example, has two federal districts—the Eastern District of Michigan and the Western District of Michigan. Federal cases require a certain jurisdictional threshold; that is, an issue under federal law and an amount in controversy of at least $75,000, or disputes between parties of different states. Decisions in federal district courts may be appealed to the U.S. Court of Appeals for the particular region (circuit) where the federal district court is located. Michigan, for example, is in the U.S. Court of Appeals for the Sixth Circuit, which also includes federal cases in the states of Ohio, Kentucky, and Tennessee. Overall, there are thirteen federal circuits, which are directly below the highest court in the land—the U.S. Supreme Court.

The U.S. Supreme Court is the final appeal for the federal system, and only a limited number of cases are accepted for review. A case may also reach the U.S. Supreme Court on appeal from a state supreme court or through the Court's original jurisdiction in a small class of cases specified in the U.S. Constitution, such as state boundary disputes. There are nine justices on the Supreme Court. Following each vacancy on the Court, a new justice is nominated by the president and confirmed by the U.S. Senate for a lifetime appointment. A U.S. Supreme Court case is decided by a majority of at least five justices. U.S. Supreme Court decisions are recorded in written opinions that set forth the ruling by the majority. At times, a U.S. Supreme Court decision will also include one or more dissenting opinions by a minority of justices who disagree with the majority opinion. The dissenting opinions are not binding precedent.

Civil Lawsuit—Typical Proceedings

A civil lawsuit begins by one party, usually through counsel, filing a document known as a complaint. The party filing the lawsuit is the plaintiff. The party being sued is the defendant. The variety of documents filed by attorneys throughout the case are called pleadings. The complaint names the parties and alleges the facts that are believed to give rise to a legal claim or causes of action, such as negligence, breach of contract, wrongful termination, and so on. There may be multiple plaintiffs or defendants in any given case. Once the defendant is served with the complaint, they must file a document known as an answer, in which the defendant admits or denies each of the allegations in the complaint. After those initial pleadings are filed, the respective parties engage in the discovery process. Discovery is the opportunity for each side to obtain relevant documents and witness testimony (depositions) from the other side prior to going to trial. Often, there are discovery disputes between the parties and counsel, which must be resolved by the court in pre-trial motions. Such motions might entail a request for an order to produce documents, provide sworn responses to written questions (interrogatories), or make a witness available for deposition.

As is noted above, most cases are settled by the parties prior to trial. Cases that do proceed to trial may be heard by a jury upon a plaintiff's request. During trial, witnesses may be called by both sides, including the parties themselves, other fact witnesses, and, if applicable, expert witnesses if the court determines that their expertise is needed under the facts and circumstances of the case. After closing statements by both sides, a jury is given time to deliberate and render a verdict. If there is no jury, a judge may rule on the case from the bench or take time to render a written opinion. After the decision of the trial court, the losing party may appeal to a higher court in accordance with the state and federal systems described above.

The document below is a copy of the original complaint filed by NFL star Reggie Bush in his negligence case arising from injuries he suffered in a game at The Edward Jones Dome in St. Louis. You will note from the first page of the complaint who are the named parties, as well as where and when the case was filed. In this case, the lawsuit was filed in January 2016 in state (circuit) court for the City of St. Louis by plaintiff Reginald Bush. The named defendants were two public entities that operated, controlled, and/or maintained the stadium where he was injured. Bush later amended the complaint to add the St. Louis Rams, LLC, as a defendant, and he ultimately won a large jury verdict against the team in that case.

COMPLAINT, REGINALD BUSH V. ST. LOUIS REGIONAL CONVENTION AND SPORTS COMPLEX AUTHORITY

1622-CC00013

In the Circuit Court of the City of St. Louis Twenty-second Judicial Circuit State of Missouri

REGINALD BUSH, **Plaintiff,** vs. **ST. LOUIS REGIONAL CONVENTION AND SPORTS COMPLEX AUTHORITY,** Serve: 901 North Broadway St. Louis, MO 63101 and **ST. LOUIS CONVENTION & VISITORS COMMISSION,** Serve: 701 Convention Plaza, Suite 300 St. Louis, MO 63101 **Defendants.**	Case No. Division: **JURY TRIAL DEMANDED**

Petition

Plaintiff Reginald Bush files this Petition against Defendants St. Louis Regional Convention and Sports Complex Authority and the St. Louis Convention & Visitors Commission.

(continued)

State of Missouri Twenty-Second Judicial Circuit, "Reginald Bush vs. St. Louis Regional Convention and Sports Complex Authority and St. Louis Convention & Visitors Commission," 2016.

Parties

1. Plaintiff Reginald Bush is a resident and citizen of California. Bush played for the USC Trojans football team from 2003 to 2005 where he enjoyed one of the greatest collegiate athletic careers of all time. The second overall pick of the New Orleans Saints in the 2006 NFL draft, Bush was part of the Saints team that won the franchise's first Super Bowl in 2010. In 2011, Mr. Bush was traded to the Miami Dolphins where he played two seasons before signing with the Detroit Lions on March 13, 2013. In 2015, Reggie signed with the San Francisco 49ers. Bush has been an explosive threat as a runner, receiver, and returner in his 10 years in the league, amassing over 9,000 total yards from scrimmage and 57 career touchdowns.
2. Defendant St. Louis Regional Convention and Sports Complex Authority ("RSA") is a body politic and corporate and a public instrumentality duly organized and existing under the laws of the State of Missouri. The RSA constructed, operates, leases, controls, owns, possesses, and maintains The Edward Jones Dome (the "Dome").
3. Defendant St. Louis Convention & Visitors Commission ("CVC") is a public body corporate and politic of the State of Missouri. The CVC maintains, operates, controls, possesses and manages the Dome.
4. RSA and CVC will be referred to collectively as "Defendants."

Venue

5. Venue is proper in this Court pursuant to MO. REV. STAT. §508.010 because Plaintiff was first injured in the City of St. Louis.

Facts

6. On November 1, 2015, the San Francisco 49ers played the St. Louis Rams at the Edward Jones Dome in St. Louis, MO.
7. At that time, the turf playing field at the Dome was surrounded by a slippery concrete surface, now known by many as the "concrete ring of death."
8. Defendants—collectively and individually—owned, operated, maintained, leased, controlled, and possessed the Dome, including the playing surface and surrounding concrete surface.
9. Reggie Bush was playing in the game as a running back for the San Francisco 49ers.
10. With approximately 5:30 left in the first quarter, Mr. Bush ran out of bounds while returning a punt.
11. After the play had concluded, and while trying to slow down out-of-bounds, Mr. Bush's momentum carried him from the turf to the concrete surface.
12. Mr. Bush slipped on the concrete surface and injured his left knee, ending his season.
13. One week prior to Mr. Bush's injury, on October 25, 2015, Josh McCown, quarterback for the Cleveland Browns, injured his shoulder after slipping on the same concrete surface.
14. Two weeks after Mr. Bush's injury, Defendants covered the concrete surface with blue rubber padding.

Count I—Premises Liability (All Defendants)

15. Plaintiff incorporates the above allegations.
16. On November 1, 2015, as described above, Mr. Bush was an invitee of Defendants.

17. Defendants were in control and possession of the Dome, including the playing field and surrounding surfaces.
18. Defendants owed a duty to the general public and specifically those invited on the field, including, but not limited to, players, coaches, trainers, media, youth football players, cheerleaders, fans, and referees to remove or warn of dangerous conditions in the Dome and to maintain the Dome, including the playing surface and surrounding areas, in a reasonably safe condition.
19. In violation of this duty, Defendants negligently permitted and maintained a dangerous condition to exist at the Dome, creating an unreasonable risk of injury to those invited on the field and surrounding surfaces, including Mr. Bush. Specifically, the turf playing field was surrounded by a slippery concrete surface. This abrupt change in surface was not reasonably safe.
20. As described above, Mr. Bush slipped and fell on the slippery concrete surface, injuring his left knee.
21. Defendants knew or by using ordinary care could have known of the dangerous condition. Indeed, just one week prior, another NFL player was injured by the same dangerous condition.
22. Defendants failed to use ordinary care to remove or warn of the dangerous condition.
23. As a direct result of Defendants' conduct described above, Mr. Bush suffered damages in the form of lost wages, medical expenses, loss of future earnings, and pain and suffering.
24. Defendants' conduct showed complete indifference to or conscious disregard for the safety of Mr. Bush and others, thereby justifying an award of punitive damages to punish Defendants and to deter Defendants and others from like conduct.

WHEREFORE, Plaintiff Reginald Bush prays for judgment against Defendants in a fair and reasonable amount in excess of twenty-five thousand dollars ($25,000.00), for punitive damages, his costs herein incurred, and for such other and further relief as may be just and proper.

Count II—Negligence (All Defendants)

25. Plaintiff incorporates the above allegations.
26. Defendants owed Mr. Bush and the general public a duty of reasonable care.
27. Defendants breached the duty owed to Mr. Bush by one or more of the following negligent acts or omissions:
    a. Designing, constructing, and/or setting up the playing field such that it was surrounded by a slippery concrete surface;
    b. Failing to cover the slippery concrete surface with padding;
    c. Failing to provide warnings related to the concrete surface; and
    d. Such further acts as will be revealed during discovery.
28. As a direct result of Defendants' conduct described above, Mr. Bush suffered damages in the form of lost wages, medical expenses, loss of future earnings, and pain and suffering.
29. Defendants' conduct showed complete indifference to or conscious disregard for the safety of Mr. Bush and others, thereby justifying an award of punitive damages to punish Defendants and to deter Defendants and others from like conduct.

(continued)

WHEREFORE, Plaintiff Reginald Bush prays for judgment against Defendants in a fair and reasonable amount in excess of twenty-five thousand dollars ($25,000.00), for punitive damages, his costs herein incurred, and for such other and further relief as may be just and proper.

//
//
//

Respectfully Submitted,
THE SIMON LAW FIRM, P.C.
By: /s/ John G. Simon
John G. Simon, #35231
Kevin M. Carnie Jr., #60979
Timothy M. Cronin, #63383
800 Market Street, Ste. 1700
St. Louis, MO 63101
jsimon@simonlawpc.com
kcarnie@simonlawpc.com
tcronin@simonlawpc.com
Phone: 314-241-2929
Fax: 314-241-2029

KINSELLA WEITZMAN ISER KUMP & ALDISERT LLP

Shawn Holley
Jeremiah Reynolds
Nick Soltman
808 Wilshire Blvd., 3rd floor
Santa Monica, CA 90401
sholley@kwikalaw.com
jreynolds@kwikalaw.com
nsoltman@kwikalaw.com
Phone: 310-566-9800
Fax: 310-566-9850

Attorneys for Plaintiff Reginald Bush

Glossary of Laws and Legal Terminology

Key laws and legal terms used throughout this text are defined below. The relevant area of law is noted in parentheses, where applicable.

- **Age Discrimination in Employment Act (ADEA) (Employment Discrimination)** This is a federal civil rights law that was passed by Congress in 1967. It prohibits employment discrimination based on age against persons 40 years of age and older.

- **Agent (Agency Law)** An agent is a representative who acts on behalf of a principal and is subject to the control of the principal. A sports agent typically acts as a representative for professional athletes and coaches to secure and negotiate endorsement contracts and employment on their behalf.
- **Americans with Disabilities Act of 1990 (ADA) (Employment and Civil Rights Law)** This is a federal statute that prohibits discrimination against qualified persons with a disability in employment (Title I), state and local government (Title II), and places of public accommodation (Title III), and imposes a duty of reasonable accommodation for the disabled in those contexts.
- **Assault (Torts and Criminal Law)** An intentional tort and/or crime that involves threat of imminent harm to another.
- **Battery (Torts and Criminal Law)** An intentional tort and/or crime that involves harmful touching of another without consent.
- **Breach of Duty (Torts)** An element of a claim for negligence that involves failure to act in a reasonable manner or failure to act in accordance with the applicable standard of care.
- **Civil Law** The body of law that relates to private claims between parties that are enforced by civil lawsuits or causes of action that seek monetary damages.
- **Compensatory Damages (Torts and Contracts)** Monetary damages awarded in tort and contract cases intended to compensate the plaintiff for actual harm.
- **Consequential Damages (Contracts)** Monetary damages awarded in contract cases for indirect economic losses incurred by the non-breaching party.
- **Criminal Law** The body of law that involves prosecution by the state or federal government for wrongful acts considered by society to violate the public peace. Most criminal laws are established by statute wherein crimes and prescribed punishments are defined by state or federal laws.
- **Disparate Treatment (Employment Discrimination)** This is one form of illegal discrimination in employment, where an employer treats similarly situated persons differently based upon characteristics that fall within a protected classification.
- **Employment at Will (Employment Law)** This is a general doctrine under common law that, absent a written contract for employment, an employer may terminate an employee at any time for any reason, subject to statutory exceptions that prohibit illegal discrimination.
- **Equal Pay Act of 1963 (Employment Discrimination)** This is a federal statute that prohibits wage discrimination based on sex in jobs that require the same skill, effort, and responsibilities performed under similar working conditions within the same organization.
- **Fair Labor Standards Act (Employment and Labor Law)** This is a federal statute that governs minimum wage and overtime requirements as well as child labor practices.
- **Gross Negligence (Torts)** A higher degree of negligence that involves extreme carelessness or reckless misconduct.
- **Jurisdiction** The formal ability of a court to exercise judicial authority over a particular legal matter.
- **Liquidated Damages (Contracts)** Monetary damages that are agreed upon by the parties in advance to be awarded to the non-breaching party in the event of a breach.
- **Negligence (Torts)** Action or inaction by a party that causes harm to another and satisfies the elements of 1) duty; 2) breach of duty; 3) causation; and 4) damages.

- **Office for Civil Rights (OCR) (Title IX, ADA)** A federal agency under the U.S. Department of Education that enforces civil rights laws prohibiting schools from discrimination based on race, sex, disability, and other protected classifications.
- **Risk Management** Organizational policies and practices that are designed to evaluate risk, protect the health and safety of constituents, and reduce liability exposure to the organization.
- **Specific Performance (Contracts)** A contract remedy wherein the court orders the breaching party to perform as promised under the contract, in lieu of an award of monetary damages.
- **Standard of Care (Torts)** The applicable duty owed by a defendant in a negligence case to act reasonably to prevent harm to others.
- **Strict Liability (Torts/Product Liability)** A standard of liability in product liability cases where a manufacturer may be liable for harm caused by defective products, regardless of intent.
- **Title VII (Employment Discrimination)** This is a federal civil rights law that was passed by Congress as part of the Civil Rights Act of 1964. It prohibits employment discrimination based on protected classifications, which include race, color, national origin, religion, and sex.
- **Title IX (Sex Discrimination in Educational Programs)** This is a federal civil rights law that was passed by Congress as part of the Education Amendments of 1972. The statute reads, "No person in the United States shall, on the basis of sex, be excluded from participation in, be denied the benefits of, or be subjected to discrimination under any education program or activity receiving Federal financial assistance."
- **Waiver and Release (Torts/Contracts)** This is a type of contract that is used by sport organizations to absolve them from liability for harm suffered by sport participants.

II. The Ethics

Ethical Concepts for Sport Managers and Participants

Overview

As with all businesses, managers in the sport industry confront ethical issues and problems. The business of sport encompasses a wide range of individuals, organizations, schools, facilities, equipment manufacturers, and other entities, who are regularly challenged by ethical decision-making. Athletes and sport participants also face ethical issues that are rooted in notions of fair play and maintaining the integrity of the game. Sports ethics, like business ethics, are focused on what is the right thing to do in sport business and in sport competition itself.

The study of ethics in general deals with the moral values and principles that govern how a person behaves or acts. Ethics is concerned with what is morally right and wrong. Ethical decision-making in sport is distinct from compliance with applicable legal requirements. As is clear in the case scenarios throughout this text, certain actions or inactions by individuals or sport organizations might be legal yet unacceptable under applicable ethical standards. Below is an overview of the contexts in which ethical considerations are prevalent in sport competition and the sport industry at large.

Ethics in Sport Competition

Athletes and coaches frequently bend the rules to gain a competitive advantage over their opponents. Often, this is a type of gamesmanship or sport strategy; however, at times it may cross the line into cheating or unethical conduct. For example, a tennis player might verbally taunt their opponent or call a ball "out" when they are unsure where it landed. Or a baseball pitcher deliberately throws an inside pitch in retaliation for "brush-back" pitches previously thrown by the opposing pitcher. Such actions violate the spirit of good sportsmanship if not the written rules of the game. Sometimes athletes push those boundaries even further to gain a competitive advantage, for example, by engaging in doping in cycling or using technology to steal signs in baseball. Those actions clearly violate the rules and standards of the game and threaten the integrity of the sport itself. Such conduct is considered unethical because it contravenes the values and moral principles applicable to sport, such as integrity and fair play.

There are many examples of a cheating culture throughout sport history, including gambling scandals in baseball and basketball, doping scandals in cycling and Olympic track and field, spying on opposing teams in the NFL, and electronic sign stealing in MLB. Some forms of cheating are blatant, while others are less overt. Some acts have been criminal-like in nature, such as the "bounty system" implemented by the New Orleans Saints that paid bonuses to team members who intentionally harmed opposing players through violence on the field. The motivation for most forms of cheating in sport can be described as simply as "winning is everything" and "the ends justify the means." Competitive sports at all levels tend to overemphasize winning, and ethical decision-making is influenced by parents, coaches, schools, or teams that subscribe to a "win at all costs" mentality. At the highest levels, cheating is motivated by prestige, commercialization, and other financial gains for individual athletes and their organizations. Sometimes, athletes succumb to cheating due to pressure by others or their own belief that cheating is necessary to "level the playing field" because "everyone else is doing it." A more ethical approach to competition is a sportsmanship model, where sport is a means to develop good character and demonstrate values of fairness, integrity, and respect (Hanson and Savage, 2012).

Youth Sports

Ethics in youth sports are of particular concern because sport has an educational mission for young people. Youth sport organizations and K–12 schools have a legal and ethical duty to educate and protect the health and safety of minors who participate. Children who play youth sports should also be taught the virtues of fairness, integrity, following the rules, and respect for others. Youth sports is not only a means to identify and train future athletes; it plays a significant role in character development, leadership, responsibility, respect, and other important moral values. A key ethical consideration in youth sports relates to the over-emphasis on winning instead of promoting fitness, team building, and fun for the benefit of all. Another ethical concern is ensuring health and safety when dealing with children whose minds and bodies are not fully developed. Youth sport organizations and K–12 schools have a special duty to protect minors from physical and mental abuse, harassment, and bullying. Ethical concerns in youth sports also extend to parents of sport participants, who sometimes intervene excessively by disputing coaching tactics or arguing with officials. This sets a bad example for their children and others, and undermines the important life lessons that can be learned through sport participation.

Intercollegiate Sports

There is much debate today over the role of college sports and their governing bodies, particularly the National Collegiate Athletic Association (NCAA). The historical model under the NCAA is one of amateurism and the primary role of college sports as an educational mission. Under this model, college athletes are "student-athletes," and the NCAA rules require amateur status, academic eligibility standards, and ethical standards for student-athletes, coaches, and institutions. Many argue this is naïve and exploitative of college athletes, who are precluded from earning money for their services as well as their own name, image, and likeness, while their schools gain enormous financial windfalls through commercialization of their teams and brands. The NCAA rules have been criticized as arbitrary, overly restrictive, and selectively enforced. Some argue that the NCAA and its member institutions are hypocritical in their adherence to an outdated and idealistic model of sports in the face of the reality that college sports are big business. These arguments have led to recent legislative changes that now permit college athletes to receive compensation from third parties for their name, image, and likeness (NIL), without jeopardizing their eligibility under NCAA amateurism rules. There are other major ethical considerations in intercollegiate sports in areas such as health and safety, eligibility issues, academic fraud, and the basic questions surrounding compensation and employment status for college athletes without compromising the stated goals of higher education.

Professional Sports

Professional sports are a billion-dollar industry with a huge following. It plays an integral part in today's culture with tremendous media and fan interest and valuable corporate sponsorships. Support for local teams and athletes helps to unite diverse groups and brings great pride to local communities. There are enormous stakes in winning and losing, in terms of economic and non-economic gains for athletes, coaches, and owners. This leads to unethical practices for the sake of "winning at all costs" as well as financial greed. Historically, there have been many cheating scandals in professional sports for unethical purposes, such as point-shaving in basketball in furtherance of illegal gambling, performance-enhancing drugs to gain a competitive advantage, and intentional violence beyond the rules of the game to deliberately harm opponents. There are also ethical debates about how to make professional sports safer for the protection of the athletes themselves, who for years were left in the dark about medical risks of traumatic brain injuries in certain contact sports. Other ethical considerations relate to diversity, equity, and inclusion of women and minorities in sport participation and coaching, to increase sport opportunities and ensure fair treatment. And finally, individual athletes have a moral responsibility as role models and citizens in their communities to conduct themselves on and off the field in a manner consistent with values of good character and respect.

Ethics in Sport Business

There is considerable overlap in sports ethics and business ethics applicable to the sport industry at large. Sport managers face ethical issues related to diversity, equity, and inclusion in the workplace, managing risk and acknowledging responsibility for failures, protecting health and safety of others, ensuring safe playing environments and working conditions, abiding by applicable industry standards, employing qualified personnel, and avoiding conflicts of interests and self-dealing.

Many segments of the sport industry face similar challenges. For example, schools and universities and professional sport teams and leagues benefit from athletic success. This includes financial, reputational, and competitive success that brings substantial money and prestige at the organizational level. Those entities that adopt an "ends justify the means" mentality are motivated to cut corners, circumvent rules or regulations, or otherwise make poor ethical choices when winning and the related financial rewards are the primary objectives. This attitude helps explain the conduct of major universities that engage in academic fraud to maintain eligibility for their star athletes, or teams and leagues that exploit their athletes by compromising their health and well-being in order to win. Ethical considerations are also disregarded in institutions or organizations that cover up negligence or sexual assaults perpetrated by athletes and athletic personnel to protect their own reputation and avoid liability. Sport organizations, including schools and institutions, often frame their ethical decision-making in a purely business context, by prioritizing money and success over professionalism, fairness, and equity. Such decisions are rarely based on considerations of what is morally right and wrong.

The sport industry also has ethical obligations to its stakeholders to engage in corporate social responsibility and help to foster a supportive environment for social justice and athlete social activism. This includes corporate sponsorships that align with good character and good causes, and initiatives to increase diversity, equity, and inclusion in the workplace. The sport industry, like many other businesses, has also historically excluded women and minorities from leadership roles, such as coaching, administration, and front office management. Sport organizations, such as schools, teams, leagues, and governing bodies, should be cognizant of this history and implement ethical standards and guidelines to promote ethical principles of fairness and inclusion to benefit their organizations and society at large.

Glossary of Ethical Concepts and Terminology

Relevant ethical concepts and terminology used throughout this text are defined below.

- **Conflict of Interest** This refers to a situation when individual or business interests conflict with those of another to whom a duty is owed.
- **Conformity Bias** This refers to those who behave like those around them rather than using their own personal judgment.
- **Consequentialism** A doctrine that the morality of an action is to be judged solely by its consequences.
- **Explicit Bias** This refers to attitudes and beliefs that people have about particular groups or persons on a conscious level.
- **Framing** This refers to the frame of reference by which we examine a particular situation.
- **Implicit Bias** This refers to an unconscious association, belief, or attitude toward particular groups or persons.
- **Incrementalism** This refers to unconsciously lowering ethical standards over time through slight changes in behavior, leading to a "slippery slope" of unethical conduct.
- **Rationalization** This refers to an excuse given to justify a failure to meet ethical standards.

- **Self-Serving Bias** This refers to someone taking credit for positive events or outcomes, but blaming outside factors for negative events or outcomes.
- **Values** These are individual beliefs about what is right and wrong that serve to guide our behavior and decisions.

Closing Arguments

Legal and ethical principles significantly impact sport and the sport industry. Legal issues and disputes consistently arise in sport settings at all levels. As a sport manager, you must know the law, appreciate legal risks, and take appropriate action to minimize harm to others and reduce the legal liability of your organization. However, merely refraining from illegal conduct is not sufficient to maintain an ethical workplace and sport environment. There are important ethical principles that must guide decision-making in sport organizations and sport competition itself. Sport managers consistently face ethical questions in various sport settings related to integrity, fairness, diversity, equity, health and safety, employment practices, financial transparency, and social justice. This is also true in sport competition at all levels, where participants should embody values and principles of sportsmanship and respect. Ethics guides the understanding of what is morally right and wrong.

Study Questions

1. What are the sources of U.S. law? Explain the key differences between civil law and criminal law.
2. Explain which parties are the plaintiff and defendant in a civil lawsuit. Why might parties to a lawsuit decide to voluntarily settle their case instead of proceeding to trial?
3. Discuss the ethics issues that are specific to youth sports, college sports, and professional sports.
4. What are the key ethical concepts pertinent to sport managers and sport organizations in general?

Sport-Related Injuries and Managing Health and Safety

CHAPTER 2

Opening Statement

Liability for negligence in sports is a relatively new concept in our U.S. legal system. Historically, courts did not favorably view legal claims asserted by sport participants who were injured in the course of play. The rationale in those early cases was that those who voluntarily engaged in physical activities should bear responsibility for any harm they incurred. Yet, over time, as more of these cases occurred, courts began to recognize that athletic competition did not exist in a vacuum, and that "some other restraints of civilization must accompany every athlete onto the playing field" (*Nabozny v. Barnhill,* 1975). The law also evolved to recognize injury claims brought by sport spectators, and consumers and users of athletic products and equipment. This chapter examines the legal aspects of sport-related injuries in those realms and the ethical aspects of risk management in sport organizations to protect the health and safety of those to whom they owe a duty of care.

Section I of this chapter addresses the fundamental legal principles of tort law. Specifically, it explains the elements of a legal claim for negligence as well as the typical sport scenarios that give rise to negligence claims. In addition, this section focuses on other possible tort claims that occur on and off the field in sport, including gross negligence, product liability, and intentional torts such as battery and assault. This section also explains the defenses that may be asserted in response to claims of negligence in sport, with particular attention to the doctrine of assumption of risk. Significantly, there are many real-life case decisions that illustrate these legal principles, and many of those cases will be identified and discussed in detail. Finally, this section explains how risk management in sport organizations is designed to reduce the likelihood of injuries and protect organizations from legal liability when injuries do occur.

Section II of this chapter addresses the ethical aspects of decision-making by schools, coaches, manufacturers, and other sport managers to protect others from health and safety risks and dangers. For example, how do schools best protect their student-athletes from harm and what types of risks are important

LEARNING OBJECTIVES

After reading this chapter, students will:

1. Understand the types of health and safety risks in sport

2. Know the elements of a legal claim based in negligence

3. Understand how the defense of assumption of risk applies in tort cases in sport

4. Recognize typical fact scenarios that give rise to tort cases in sport

5. Consider the ethical implications of risk management in schools, sport organizations, and product manufacturing

6. Understand the legal and ethical issues surrounding the handling of serious injury cases in sport

7. Recognize the ethical failures in institutional cover-ups and denial of responsibility

to recognize and analyze? Further, what is the appropriate course of action to be taken by a coach or administrator if a high degree of risk is present in a particular sport or activity? Is it ethical for an administrator to frame their school's response to personal injuries from a business perspective, or by prioritizing team success, rather than acknowledging responsibility? What are the aspects of ethical decision-making for companies that manufacture and sell sports equipment and protective gear? Ultimately, what ethical message is sent when schools, sport organizations, or manufacturers rely primarily on financial projections and potential legal exposure when developing and implementing their risk management policies?

I. The Law

Tort Law: Fundamentals

Overview

A tort is a wrong or injury suffered as a result of another's action or inaction. Torts are based in civil law. Torts are distinct from crimes because criminal law involves prosecution by the state or federal government to punish or imprison offenders. Under tort law, the injured party (the "plaintiff") may sue the party they believe is legally responsible (the "defendant") in a civil action to recover monetary damages as compensation for the injury. Lawsuits alleging tortious conduct are very frequently resolved ("settled") voluntarily between the parties with a payment of money in exchange for a dismissal of the legal action. However, cases that are not settled will proceed to trial before a jury. At the conclusion of all the evidence at trial, the assigned judge will instruct the jury on how to apply the law and the jury will decide whether or not the defendant is liable (the term for civil responsibility) and, if so, the amount of damages to be awarded to the plaintiff.

This section examines four general categories of torts that are common in sport: negligence, gross negligence, product liability, and intentional torts. For each category, the elements necessary to establish a cause of action (also referred to as a "claim") are identified and discussed in detail.

Negligence

The claim of negligence arises from an act or omission that results in injury to another. Negligence involves unintentional conduct where a defendant causes harm to another but did not intend to do so. Negligence cases are extremely common in the realm of sports because there is often a risk of injury associated with athletic competition and recreational activities. For example, a sport participant or spectator might be injured during a competition due to a facility owner's failure to properly maintain the premises or warn of dangerous conditions. An individual might be injured by athletic equipment that was unreasonably dangerous or defective when manufactured and sold to the user. A student-athlete might be harmed due a school's failure to render appropriate medical attention when an injury occurred. Or injuries might result when a school or coach fails to properly supervise their team practice or conducts workouts that exceed recommended training or conditioning standards. Note that in each of these examples there was no intent to cause injury to others, but injuries occurred nonetheless because of the defendant's conduct. This is sometimes characterized as "ordinary negligence," as distinct from "gross negligence," which is described further below.

The required elements of a claim for negligence are (a) duty, (b) breach of duty, (c) causation, and (d) damages (Spengler et al., 2016). A plaintiff must prove all four elements to recover monetary damages from the defendant in a negligence case. Each element is described further in the subsections below.

Duty (Standard of Care)

A plaintiff must show that the defendant owed a certain duty or standard of care to protect others. In sport cases based in negligence, a duty or responsibility commonly exists on the part of an individual, school, sport manager, or organization to sport participants and spectators. For example, they must provide a reasonably safe premises and safe environment for those who might be injured in athletic activities and competition. Or a sport organization or governing body has rules, regulations, or bylaws that create a sport-specific standard of care. In some instances, a duty may exist by virtue of state and federal laws or local ordinances. Also, industry standards or community practices might establish the duty of care in a negligence action. And certain special relationships automatically give rise to a duty in sport-related negligence cases, such as the responsibility of coaches to their athletes to protect them from unreasonable risk of harm, or athletic medicine personnel who have a duty to render prompt medical aid to players or student-athletes under their care.

Breach of Duty

Once a duty or standard of care is established, the plaintiff must prove the second element of negligence, which is known as a breach of duty. The injured party must show that the defendant's action, or inaction, failed to meet the applicable standard of care in the particular circumstances. For example, a baseball team owner commits a breach of duty if they fail to provide protective fencing or netting behind the plate and someone is injured by a foul ball in that open-seating area. A breach of duty may exist when an umpire fails to stop a youth soccer game during severe weather conditions, leading to injuries on the field. Or a facility owner and sport league fail to provide adequate lighting during scheduled outdoor night games, and injuries result from the lack of visibility. Other common breaches of duty in sport might be found if a fitness club does not maintain a safe premises for its members who participate in onsite fitness classes; a school fails to render medical aid to a student-athlete who collapses on the field of play; or a sport league issues unsafe equipment to its league participants. The existence of a breach of duty will depend upon the specific facts and circumstances of each case. To determine if this element is satisfied, it is necessary to examine whether the defendant's acts or omissions fell below a certain standard of care, and thereby created an unreasonable risk of harm to the injured party.

Causation

The third element that must be proven in a negligence case is causation. It is necessary to show a link between the defendant's actions and the injury that occurred. The term "cause in fact" refers to a more direct form of causation where it is established that the defendant's acts or omissions were the factual cause of the plaintiff's injuries. Courts sometimes explain this as a "but for" rule; that is, but for the defendant's conduct, the plaintiff would not have been injured. The term "proximate cause" is used to describe more indirect causation that in many jurisdictions will satisfy the causation element. This relies on the concept of foreseeability, meaning that the injury was the natural and probable result of the breach of duty and that the defendant knew or reasonably should have known that harm could occur.

Damages

The fourth element of a negligence claim is that actual harm or injury occurred. This is known as damages. Damages might take many different forms. For example, an injured party who cannot return to work will suffer economic damages in the form of their ongoing medical expenses and wage loss. That same individual might also lose their future earning capacity as a result of the particular injury, which is another type of economic loss. There are also damages associated with physical pain and suffering incurred from the injury. And while physical injury alone will satisfy this fourth element of negligence, it is notable that with many physical injuries there can also be accompanying emotional harm or distress, such as anxiety, depression, humiliation, or embarrassment. These are known as non-economic losses, and they are also recoverable in a lawsuit based in negligence. A plaintiff who successfully proves their negligence claim is entitled to an award of monetary damages from a jury to compensate them for their economic losses and mental distress. Taken together, these are known as compensatory damages, and the specific amount of the award is determined by the jury, based on the evidence presented at trial.

> **Case Notes:** *Baker-Goins v. First Baptist School of Charleston*
>
> Despite recent developments in concussion protocols for high school contact sports, there are many instances where such protocols are not properly followed and serious injury results. In 2013, Brett Baker-Goins, a student-athlete at First Baptist School of Charleston, suffered his first sports-related concussion in a school basketball game. Brett did not have medical clearance to return to play, but re-entered the season prematurely and suffered another concussion, the second one resulting in permanent traumatic brain injury. The school was expected to follow the South Carolina Independent School Association's (SCISA) return-to-play protocol, which had guidelines regarding the proper medical clearance needed for an athlete to safely return to his/her sport following a concussion.
>
> A negligence action was filed on behalf of Brett seeking compensation for his injuries. It was alleged that the school rushed him back to athletic activities too quickly, resulting in his second, more severe brain injury. The guidelines specifically provided that schools remove an athlete from play after a concussion, have the athlete's symptoms and condition reviewed by a medical professional, inform and educate the parents, and keep the player out of further action until cleared by a medical professional. At trial, the plaintiff argued that the school failed to follow the SCISA guidelines with respect to medical clearance and a safe return to play, and the school did not take proper precautions to protect him.
>
> The return-to-play protocol set forth by the SCISA was consistent with South Carolina state law and similar to many high school practices across the country. Since 2009, many states have adopted youth concussion laws, which address these same circumstances involving a premature return to play. Often young athletes are pressured to shake off injuries and return to the game before they are ready, leading to further injury with more severe consequences. With concussions, a second injury is referred to as second-impact syndrome. Second-impact syndrome can happen when a second concussion occurs before the first has

healed. Yet five weeks after his first concussion, when Brett returned to play, he did not have proper medical clearance. He suffered traumatic brain injury after his second concussion, showing that he had not fully healed from the first concussion. Had the school followed protocol and obtained medical clearance for Brett, he would have sat out longer, which could have saved him from the mental and physical harm caused by second-impact syndrome.

As to duty, the lawsuit alleged that the coaches and the athletic department, including athletic medicine personnel at the school, owed a duty to protect the athletes and their safety, especially as they were minors. Regarding the necessary element of causation, it was alleged that the plaintiff's second concussion would not have occurred but for the school's failure to follow protocol; that is, a cause-in-fact on the part of the school.

At the conclusion of trial in 2018, the jury found that the school's failure to follow SCISA guidelines resulted in Brett's injury, thus making the school liable for negligence. The jury awarded the plaintiff $5.87 million in compensatory damages. Though money will not resolve the permanent harm suffered by Brett Baker-Goins, his case did draw national attention, and emphasizes the importance of safety protocols in youth and high school sports and recreation. Schools are held responsible to provide proper education, prevention, and treatment for concussions and must adhere to medical protocols.

Vicarious Liability

Sport-related negligence actions frequently involve named defendants whose responsibility is derived from their ability to control the actions of the negligent party. This principle is known as vicarious liability. It is a form of liability that arises from an agency relationship between the negligent actor and another party. The most common example is an employer/employee relationship. An employer may be found vicariously liable for the negligent acts of their employees that were committed in the scope of their employment. The employer, as defendant, may be found liable if their employee was authorized to do an act but did so in a negligent manner.

The doctrine of vicarious liability is often invoked in negligence cases involving high school and college sport participants. In such cases, the student may have suffered injuries caused by the negligent act of their coach or their team's medical personnel. In a subsequent lawsuit, the injured high school student will name the school district as a defendant on the theory of vicarious liability. Similarly, injured student-athletes in college will sue their university based on this doctrine. Typically, coaches, aides, teachers, custodians, trainers, and administrators are viewed as agents of the school, and the district or university will be liable if the alleged negligent acts occurred in the course of employment. In *Eddy v. Syracuse University* (1980), a group of students from another school were not authorized to use the defendant's facilities; however, they were admitted into the locked gym by a custodian who was a university employee. One student was then injured in the gym when he ran into a glass door while playing ultimate frisbee. While the university would not have owed a duty to the students from another school, they were responsible for the negligent acts of their employee.

Schools and universities also have a direct duty to supervise and provide proper instruction in classes, such as physical education, which involve risk of physical injuries. This is distinct from their vicarious responsibility. In *Eddy*, there was also a jury question as to whether the school itself was negligent for installing glass doors in a gym, with close proximity to court sidelines, as it constituted a dangerous condition. Similar circumstances arose in *DeMauro v. Tusculum College, Inc.* (1980), when a first-year physical education student was injured in a golf class. The injury resulted from an inexperienced student teaching assistant demonstrating a golf shot in class, which unfortunately struck and harmed the student. The court stated that the physical education professor and the college owed a duty of proper supervision and instruction to their students, which was breached by delegating their duty to an inexperienced assistant who had been placed in a position of sole responsibility for the class.

Case Notes: *Mileto v. Sachem Central School District*

In the summer of 2017, Joshua Mileto was a 16-year-old junior at Sachem East High School and a member of the school football team. During a pre-season workout drill, Joshua was struck in the head by a 400-pound log. Joshua and four other teammates were instructed by their coaches to carry the heavy log together on their shoulders as part of a summer training drill. The drill was modeled after a Navy SEAL exercise that has been used to train an elite, highly trained and conditioned military unit. The incident led to Joshua's death and also caused severe emotional trauma for his teammates who witnessed it. A wrongful death lawsuit was filed by Joshua's parents against two defendants, the Sachem Central School District and the Sachem East Touchdown Club Inc., which ran the preseason camp. The rules and regulations of the New York Public High School Athletic Association (NYPHSAA) apply to this case, which focused on the nature of the practice drill and whether it was reasonable and appropriate for high school athletes. In a separate lawsuit against the school district, Joshua's teammates sought damages due to the lack of mental health resources provided by the school to assist them in coping with the loss of their friend and teammate (*Paolucci v. Sachem Central School District, 2018*). The school district conducted an internal investigation and made personnel changes by reassigning the head and assistant football coaches to different positions.

The Mileto family sought $15 million in damages. Their lawsuit claimed that Joshua died due to the negligence and carelessness of the defendants in utilizing these drills that were not suitable for young athletes. Joshua was 5-foot-6 and 134 pounds at the time of the incident. It was also alleged that the team had not been properly instructed on how to perform the drill, and that officials failed to supervise the activity and provide Joshua with proper medical care. The school district claimed that they were not responsible because the summer training camp was run by a booster group, not the high school. However, it is undisputed that the workout drill took place on school grounds and was conducted by school staff.

In March 2021, the case was reportedly settled for a seven-figure sum, to be used by the family for academic and athletic scholarships in memory of Joshua Mileto. The circumstances of this tragic death send a strong message to school districts that coaches and athletic departments have a responsibility to young athletes to ensure that their training is safe and age appropriate, and that student health and well-being must be a top priority over competitive success.

Defenses to Negligence

There are many legal defenses that may be asserted when defending against negligence claims. The primary and most common defenses in sport-related negligence cases are assumption of risk and comparative negligence. A plaintiff must first satisfy all the requisite elements of a negligence claim as set forth above. If they do so, then the defendant must come forward with their defenses to avoid liability.

Assumption of Risk

Assumption of risk is a legal defense that is frequently raised in negligence cases brought by participants or spectators against facility owners, team owners, leagues, and sport organizations. It involves the voluntary assumption, express or implied, of known and appreciated risks or dangers. This defense has three required elements: (a) the risk is inherent to the sport; (b) the plaintiff voluntarily consented to exposure to the risk; and (c) the plaintiff knew, understood, and appreciated inherent risks or dangers (Spengler et al., 2016).

In sports and recreational activities, there are many inherent risks that are ordinary risks associated with the game. For example, in ice hockey, there are obvious dangers in skating at a high speed with others in a confined rink, using sticks as equipment, and shooting hard pucks into nets. Those risks are inherent to the game and hockey players voluntarily consent to those potential dangers, including occasional physical contact, when they choose to participate. If a hockey player is injured from those ordinary risks of the game, or a spectator who knowingly attends a professional hockey game is injured by a loose puck, the defense of the facility or team owner in a negligence case would be that the plaintiff assumed the risk of their own injuries. The third element, however, might not be satisfied if the participant is a minor incapable of understanding and appreciating the risks or dangers of the game. Spectators as well as participants are typically found to assume only those risks that are related to the game and are also obvious and foreseeable.

Assumption of risk is not necessarily an absolute defense against claims brought by athletes or spectators in inherently dangerous sports. It must first be determined whether the injury was the result of an ordinary risk in the sport. For example, in a negligence case filed against an NFL team, the plaintiff was a professional football player who was injured during the course of the game when he ran out of bounds and skidded on a concrete surface adjacent to the playing field, causing serious injury to his knee. In that case, the risk of harm presented by the concrete surface was not an ordinary risk of the game of football. A plaintiff does not assume the risk of violation of standards by the team or stadium operator, as it is not an inherent risk of the game of football. In that case, the jury found in favor of the plaintiff on his claim of negligence based in premises liability and awarded judgment in his favor and against the team in the amount of $12.5 million. The jury concluded that the team negligently permitted and maintained a dangerous condition to exist in the stadium, thereby creating an unreasonable risk of injury to the players (*Bush v. St. Louis Rams, LLC,* 2018).

There are many examples of spectators who are injured while attending a game. In negligence cases arising from those injuries, the doctrine of assumption of risk might apply if the plaintiff knowingly exposed themselves to risk of harm by choosing to sit close to action in unprotected seating. There is a long line of negligence cases filed by baseball fans who were injured when they were struck by a foul ball at the ballpark. In such cases filed against team owners, the courts have established what is known as a limited duty, requiring team owners to provide seats protected by screens or netting behind the plate and extending down the first and third base lines, in sufficient numbers as may reasonably be expected for fans to purchase. It is generally held that a spectator who has knowledge of the game and chooses an unprotected seat will assume the risk of injury by a foul ball. In those types of cases, a team owner fulfills their limited duty and will not be found liable if they had a sufficient number of protected seats available for the spectators (See, e.g., *Benejam v. Detroit Tigers, Inc.,* 2001).

Comparative Negligence

Comparative negligence is a defense that is based on the allocation of fault between parties. This entails a comparison by the jury of the respective fault between plaintiff and defendant, and among multiple defendants. Most states have adopted some form of comparative negligence, except for just a few states that adhere to an old doctrine where a plaintiff may not recover damages if they contributed to their own injuries. Under pure comparative negligence, each defendant is only liable for their own percentage of fault, as determined by a jury. Under that analysis, an award of damages to the plaintiff is also reduced by the degree to which the plaintiff is at fault. For example, if a jury finds that a defendant is negligent, but that the plaintiff is 40% responsible for their own injuries, then the total damage award to the plaintiff would be reduced by that percentage.

> **Case Notes: *Martin v. The Regents of the University of California***
>
> During the 2017–18 academic year, Melissa Martin was a member of the cheerleading team at the University of California–Berkeley (UC Berkeley). Despite her student-athlete status on the team, Martin raised claims against the school that she and her teammates were treated more like "half-letes" by the university, especially in terms of medical and safety priorities, when compared to male athletes (Otero-Amad, 2019). Martin suffered three concussions in her time on the team and claimed that she did not receive sufficient care from her coaches or medical advisors to properly treat her injuries. From November 2017 to January 2018, Martin continued to suffer from concussion symptoms that affected her everyday habits, like studying and academics. Martin resigned from the team in February 2018. Though she had been medically cleared to participate at that point, she was not free from concussion symptoms, and eventually withdrew from UC Berkeley as a student because of her post-concussion syndrome, which persisted in the summer and into the fall semester. Though the university and the sport governing body claim to have protocols to treat concussions and protect their athletes, Martin claims that she was bullied by coaches into participation after her first injury, which resulted in more severe injuries (Graham, 2019).
>
> Plaintiff Martin sued multiple defendants, alleging negligence on the part of UC Berkeley, the sport governing body USA Cheer, and her coaches. Each owed a duty to protect the health and safety of their athletes, which was allegedly breached. Martin also claims that the school was negligent in retaining her coaches after she notified the athletic department about her mistreatment. In addition, although UC Berkeley did have concussion protocol in its athletic programs, it was not implemented in the cheerleading program, which was an alleged violation of California education codes and the student-athlete bill of rights. There are other legal and ethical concerns raised by the fact that men's sports often receive more attention than women's sports on concussion safety and prevention. Head injuries and severity vary from sport to sport, and there are differences in head size and neck strength between men and women that can impact sport-related head trauma, reporting, and treatment. Martin's case, which did not go to trial, is an important reminder that schools should re-examine and strictly follow concussion protocol in all sports, men's and women's, including cheerleading, which poses a high risk for female student-athletes.

Gross Negligence

In some tort cases, there is a high degree of negligence that might constitute gross negligence. Gross negligence involves a heightened degree of negligence, sometimes referred to as reckless misconduct. In such instances, while the harm itself was unintentional, the defendant intended to do the act that caused the harm and did so in a reckless manner, beyond the level of what is often called ordinary negligence.

A well-known sport case involving allegations of gross negligence arose in the context of an NFL game (*Hackbart v. Cincinnati Bengals, Inc.,* 1979). In that case, a player was injured during the game by an opposing player, who intentionally hit the back of the plaintiff's head in frustration at the conclusion of a play. The plaintiff suffered serious neck injuries and sued the opposing player and his team. The trial court found that the player acted out of anger and frustration but without a specific intent to injure, a form of recklessness akin to gross negligence, as distinct from intentional torts like assault and battery.

In Michigan, gross negligence involves conduct so reckless as to demonstrate a substantial lack of concern for whether injury results and may be shown by proof of a willful disregard for precautions or measures to attend to safety. In a recreational activity case that examined the enforceability of a waiver for ordinary negligence, the Michigan Court of Appeals held that evidence that an employee of a rock climbing facility knew that the plaintiff was wearing his safety harness backwards, and nevertheless allowed him to climb the wall, telling him to "just let go" when he was at the top of the wall, was sufficient evidence to allow a jury to decide whether the employee and facility were liable for the plaintiff's injuries caused by gross negligence (*Alvarez v. LTF Club Operations Co., Inc. d/b/a Lifetime Fitness Center,* unpublished Michigan Court of Appeals case #328221, 2016).

Product Liability

A legal claim based in product liability arises when a product causes injury to the user. In sport-related injury cases, product liability claims are common when injury results from defectively designed or unreasonably dangerous athletic equipment or protective gear, such as face masks or helmets. Manufacturers, distributors, and sellers of sports equipment and protective gear could potentially be liable as defendants in such cases. There are three typical theories on which product liability may be based: negligence, breach of warranty, and strict liability. Each is discussed further below.

Negligence Theory

Negligence could be asserted as a basis for liability in a product case regardless of the alleged defect. As in all negligence cases, the plaintiff must establish each of the requisite elements of duty, breach, causation, and damages. With a negligence theory, the plaintiff must show that the manufacturer or other parties acted unreasonably in the creation or sale of the product, and that it caused injury to the user. Manufacturers also have a duty to warn consumers of dangers that are inherent in reasonable use of the product, including foreseeable misuse.

Breach of Warranty Theory

A breach of warranty, express or implied, is a contractual remedy. A consumer or user who is injured by a product might be able to assert that there was a written or oral representation that the product was safe for all uses. There are also implied warranties under article 2 of the Uniform Commercial Code (UCC), which nearly all states have adopted to cover the sale of consumer goods. The UCC warranties flow with the sale of the goods and they extend to include implied warranties of merchantability and fitness for a particular purpose (Spengler et al., 2016).

Strict Liability Theory

The theory of strict liability in product cases does not require satisfaction of the elements of negligence. Instead, the injured party needs to show that the product was defective when it left the manufacturer or seller, and that the defect caused the injuries. A plaintiff in a strict liability case must also demonstrate that the product was unreasonably dangerous because of the defect and that it was not substantially modified since the time of sale. Strict liability is found regardless of a determination of fault, as plaintiffs do not need to establish that the manufacturer acted unreasonably.

> **Case Notes:** *Filler v. Rayex Corporation*
>
> This product liability case was filed on behalf of a 16-year-old high school athlete who was seriously injured by defective sunglasses manufactured by the defendant. The plaintiff alleged the three different theories of product liability described above. The plaintiff was wearing flip-down baseball sunglasses during practice. While catching pop fly balls, he lost one ball in the sun and it struck him in the sunglasses. The right lens shattered, sending sharp splinters in his eye. Tragically, the young man lost his eye nine days after the incident.
>
> The three claims asserted against the manufacturer were implied warranty, negligence, and strict liability. The court ruled that the defendant was liable for breach of an implied warranty of fitness for a particular purpose because the buyer coach had relied on the fact that these sunglasses would be suitable for his high school baseball team, yet it was found that they lacked safety features of plastic or shatterproof glass. Also, the thinness of the lenses was a manufacturing defect that made the product unreasonably dangerous and the defendant strictly liable.

Intentional Torts

An intentional tort is a wrongful act that causes harm but, unlike negligence, the act was committed with intent. This means the individual who caused injury intended the consequences of their action or knew with substantial certainty that injury would occur. Intentional acts causing harm to athletes, officials, and spectators are common in sport. Usually, such incidents are considered rules violations and are handled by a league or sport governing body by imposing discipline, such as suspensions or fines. However, intentional torts can be the basis of a civil legal action for monetary damages.

Two distinct intentional torts that cause harm to persons are assault and battery. Under criminal law, assault and battery are also crimes that may be prosecuted by state or local authorities. In a civil context, however, assault and battery in sport can give rise to an action to recover money damages by the injured plaintiff against the defendant who committed the act(s). For example, fights and brawls in professional sports or physical attacks on referees or fans have sometimes been the basis for legal actions filed by the injured party to recover monetary damages for physical and emotional harm and economic losses.

Assault and battery are frequently associated together; however, each is a separate intentional tort. The necessary elements to prove the intentional torts of assault and battery are described below.

Assault

Assault is defined as the threat of harmful or offensive touching. This differs from the common usage of the term assault, which usually implies physical contact. However, by legal definition, assault is the threat of battery. A plaintiff who alleges assault in a civil case must show that the defendant had intent that caused apprehension of battery, apparent ability to commit battery, and resulting damages.

Battery

Battery is the intentional, harmful, or offensive touching of another that is unprivileged and unpermitted. A plaintiff who alleges battery in a civil case must show that the defendant had intent to contact and engaged in harmful or offensive touching that caused injury or damages. "Unprivileged" means that there was no legal right to commit the act, such as consent to strike another in the sport of boxing, or legal self-defense. The last required element is that the act was unpermitted by the plaintiff.

The typical defendants in civil assault and battery claims in a sport context are the party who committed the act and the team or organization that employs them. A well-known case example involving intentional torts in professional hockey was the lawsuit filed by Steve Moore, then a forward with the Colorado Avalanche, against Todd Bertuzzi and the Vancouver Canucks L.P. over an on-the-ice physical attack committed by Bertuzzi. Moore suffered severe neck and head injuries and his hockey career was ended. In that civil case, the plaintiff sought $68 million in damages for past and future wage loss and punitive damages. Bertuzzi was also charged criminally with assault under Canadian law. The civil case was settled many years later, just prior to trial, for an undisclosed amount (*Moore v. Bertuzzi,* 2006).

Managing Risk

As a sport manager, you must develop plans and policies to manage risk. This is critical for two key reasons: to reduce the probability of injuries, and to protect your organization from legal liability for tort claims. Ideally, sport managers should prioritize the health and safety of all to whom a duty of care is owed. But from a business standpoint, sport managers must also be cognizant of the risk of financial and reputational loss to their organization when they are sued for negligently or intentionally causing harm to others. Risk management entails the process of recognizing and analyzing all types of risks and taking the appropriate course of action to prevent them. In doing so, sport managers can effectuate policies to accomplish the dual purpose of promoting health and safety above all else and protecting their organization from legal exposure.

Risk recognition in sport is often obvious, for example, hazardous playing conditions such as slippery gym floors or uneven field turf, unsafe equipment or protective gear, or severe weather conditions at game time. Identifying these risks is important and usually involves routine inspections and common sense. Analyzing the risks means an assessment of the likelihood of serious injury. In football, for example, conducting team practice in excessive heat conditions could pose a serious risk of injury to athletes. Failing to regularly inspect and maintain a playing field or court surface could similarly lead to injuries to participants and officials. Upon analyzing and evaluating potential risks, sport managers should develop and implement a specific course of action or risk management plan. This might include making no changes (retention), taking action to reduce the risk (warnings or inspections), transferring the risk (waivers or contracts with others), or eliminating the risk altogether (avoidance by closing facilities or cancelling high-risk events). Specific plans for crisis management are also necessary, as well as emergency action plans in the event of medical emergencies.

An example of failed risk management procedures occurred in the tragic death of a varsity athlete at Gettysburg College. In that case, a 20-year-old lacrosse player collapsed during his team's fall practice. Team practice was conducted at a field without any radio, cell phone, or other communication device on hand. The school did not assign any athletic trainers to fall practice, and the assistant coach and head coach were not certified in CPR. Overall, the school lacked any sound emergency action plan to assess injury and ensure that prompt medical attention was provided to injured student-athletes. The young man died during the substantial delay in securing proper medical aid. While the school claimed that his death was not foreseeable, the court disagreed and found that the obvious risks of injuries in the sport mandates that reasonable preventive measures should have been implemented by the school and its coaches, who owed a duty to their student-athletes to protect their health and safety (*Kleinknecht v. Gettysburg College*, 1993).

Setting a Precedent

- *Nabozny v. Barnhill*
- *Bush v. St. Louis Rams, LLC*
- *Eddy v. Syracuse University*
- *Bearman v. University of Notre Dame*
- *Benejam v. Detroit Tigers, Inc.*
- *DeMauro v. Tusculum College, Inc.*
- *Hackbart v. Cincinnati Bengals, Inc.*
- *Filler v. Rayex Corporation*
- *Stringer v. Minnesota Vikings Football Club, LLC*
- *Kleinknecht v. Gettysburg College*
- *Moore v. Bertuzzi*

II. The Ethics

Case Scenarios

Case 1: *You are a college athletic director at Major U. Your school has an exclusive contract with MLAX Corp., a new company that furnishes men's lacrosse uniforms, equipment, and helmets to schools and universities. Your head* men's lacrosse coach comes to you with a request from his star player, Sam. Sam wants to wear the lacrosse helmet he wore in high school because he says it feels more comfortable and secure and he feels safer wearing it. Privately, Sam told his coach that he thinks his high school helmet looks cool and is much more popular than the MLAX brand. Sam's high school helmet was manufactured by XYZ Lacrosse, which is a direct competitor of MLAX. Major U.'s contract with MLAX requires that all players wear MLAX uniforms, equipment, and protective headgear, and includes a substantial bonus payment for Major U if there is 100% compliance. Should the athletic director authorize the equipment exception for Sam?

Case 1 presents both a legal and ethical dilemma that might occur in a college athletic program that has a contract with a major athletic brand to furnish uniforms and equipment. The manufacturer will pay large sums, sometimes millions of dollars, to the school for an exclusive agreement such as the one described in this scenario. Coaches and athletic administrators in intercollegiate athletics regularly confront ethical decision-making related to health and safety of student-athletes, including this situation, which presents a potential conflict for the school. Preventing injuries and ensuring the health and safety of the student-athlete may be at odds with the contractual obligation and the competitive and/or financial success in their athletic team or program. While we would hope that health and safety is the utmost priority, some sport managers and administrators have clouded ethical judgment that may lead to tragic outcomes when compromises are made, and when money and success are valued over health and safety. In this scenario, the school also has contractual obligations that must be adhered to receive a lucrative financial reward, which is unethical if it does not allow for health and safety exceptions.

The ethical concept of framing applies to this situation. Framing applies when people omit ethical considerations from their frame of reference and focus only on material goals, such as victory in sports or financial gain. If the athletic director focused only on the 100% compliance requirement to receive the bonus payment, they would be prioritizing money and a successful corporate partnership over student-athlete safety. The coach and student-athlete also face ethical decision-making, including this coach, who appears to want to accede to the demands of his star player, in spite of countervailing contractual obligations for the school, and doubts his student-athlete's real reasons for requesting a different helmet. While safety should be first and foremost in this decision-making process, there are competing interests in play between the athletic director, who is pressured to achieve financial success in their athletic program, and the coach and student-athlete, who want team and individual success on the playing field.

Case 2: You are a new marketing representative at a major sports equipment company, SADIDA. You are assigned to a big customer/client, University "X." You have responsibility to oversee that men's football at X complies with its exclusive clothing and equipment deal with SADIDA. There is a rumor that 10 football student-athletes at X plan to tape the outside of their SADIDA football cleats during a nationally televised game, a practice commonly referred to as "spatting." The tape is wrapped around the players' ankles, which they say provides additional support during competition. However, the tape-wrapping covers the SADIDA logo that is otherwise prominent on the football cleats. It is believed that student-athletes like the way spatting looks and it has become somewhat of a fashion statement. You follow all the X football players on social media and noticed dozens of spatting photos posted with positive comments about this new look. Do you bring this spatting issue to the attention of your manager at SADIDA and, if so, what do you recommend?

Case 2 is common example of ethical issues in college football arising from relationships with corporate brands and sponsors. From the corporate standpoint, SADIDA wants and expects maximum exposure for its brand through its affiliation with University X. Your obligations and duties as a SADIDA employee include following through by all legal and ethical means to accomplish that. Your discovery and awareness of the spatting trend from social media makes it obvious that your customer's student-athletes do not necessarily have legitimate health and safety reasons to cover the SADIDA logos. In fact, from a contractual perspective, their actions might rise to the level of a breach of University X's obligations. On the other hand, you want to maintain goodwill and rapport with the football athletes and their large social media following, many of whom are your peers. Your duty of loyalty to your employer should take precedence here, by reporting what might be a circumvention or breach of the customer's contract obligations. At the same time, if health and safety is truly an issue with the SADIDA football cleats, then that must also be reported and fully investigated so that the company implements proper risk management measures, corrects any design or manufacturing defects, and issues warnings wherever applicable. Those steps would serve the dual risk management purposes of reducing the likelihood of injuries and protecting your organization from liability exposure.

Case 3: *BLUE College wanted to increase football ticket sales and generate more student interest and revenue from its athletic program. They sponsored "Rush the Field Day" for a big rivalry football game. Students who bought tickets were allowed to run on the field and climb the goalposts if BLUE won the game. BLUE did win and several students were injured when they were trampled on as the crowd ran onto the field. One student was seriously injured when he climbed the goalposts and fell to the ground. At the post-game press conference, the athletic director (AD) at BLUE wished a quick recovery to all students who were hurt in what he called a "freak accident." He emphasized that the game was a tremendous financial success for BLUE and that football ticket sales and fan enthusiasm were at an all-time high. He also announced plans to sponsor "Rush the Court Day" at BLUE, a similar event for students, to promote men's basketball.*

Case 3 is a scenario that presents legal liability issues as well as poor ethical decision-making on the part of BLUE and its AD. The "Rush the Field" event led to serious injuries caused by the negligence of the school and its administrators. It is clear that there were insufficient risk management measures—such as security and warnings to students—to prevent the likelihood of injuries from an unruly crowd. It was also foreseeable that students in that situation might get hurt while shaking or climbing goalposts in celebration of a big win. The school's express encouragement of that conduct as part of the event might rise to the level of gross negligence or reckless misconduct.

From an ethical standpoint, by characterizing the harm as a "freak accident" in the press conference, the AD failed to acknowledge any responsibility for the harm that this event caused to BLUE's students. In addition, by emphasizing the financial success and fan enthusiasm for the event, the AD prioritized money over the health and safety of students to whom they owed a duty of care. That frame of reference in the AD's statement was unethical, and the poor decision-making was reinforced by the announcement that BLUE planned to host another similar event in basketball. The best risk management course of action in this scenario is avoidance—that is, elimination of the risk, by cancelling the event.

There are two case examples in college football that involved facts similar to this scenario. At Ball State University (BSU), in October 2001, a BSU student was severely injured while attending the school's home football game. Near the end of the fourth quarter, in an imminent upset victory, BSU suggested to the fans that they climb or tear down the aluminum goalposts by flashing "The goalposts look lonely" on the scoreboard. That led to a large crowd rushing the field to celebrate the win. The BSU student jumped up to grab the goalpost, but missed, and while he was walking away, the goalpost fell on his back, rendering him a paraplegic. The student filed a lawsuit against BSU alleging gross negligence, and the case was later settled by BSU (*Bourne v. Gilman*, 2006). The obvious legal and ethical lesson in that case is that a sport organization should never actively encourage unruly or dangerous behavior that can lead to injuries to participants or spectators. Fan celebrations often lead to loss of crowd control, and it is foreseeable that serious injuries might occur as a result. In the interest of health and safety, schools would be well-advised not to permit any unauthorized persons on the field or court at the conclusion of a game.

A second example occurred in 2010, involving the tragic death of a student-employee during football practice at the University of Notre Dame. In that case, Declan Sullivan was a team videographer whose job entailed filming football practice from a scissor-lift that could be extended to heights as high as 40 feet (*University of Notre Dame*, 2011). Those lifts, however, are not recommended for use in wind conditions beyond 25 miles per hour. During severe weather conditions in South Bend, involving high winds, the head coach decided to practice outdoors. In doing so, the student was required to do his job from dangerous heights. The student himself realized the danger by sarcastically tweeting "Gusts of wind up to 60 mph today will be fun at work ... I guess I've lived long enough" before going up on the lift to do his job. Tragically, the lift toppled over in the high winds, believed to be over 45 miles per hour, and the student was killed. The athletic director had been at the practice himself when the incident occurred. He told the media that this was a "freak accident" and he did not know who was responsible. The head coach said he decided to practice outdoors because the conditions, although windy, were not unlike conditions his teams had faced before, although there were reports these were the strongest winds in the Midwest in 70 years. The ethical implications of the statements of the AD and head coach show an utter disregard for health and safety of Declan Sullivan and others associated with the ND football program. The coach's comments were framed from the perspective that this outdoor practice was necessary and advisable to toughen up his players. With regard to the AD's comments, this clearly was not a freak accident; it could easily have been anticipated and should have been prevented by moving practice indoors. Some called for the firing of both the AD and head coach, based on their negligence and their statements that appeared to emphasize football success over a student-employee's safety and welfare. The family of Declan Sullivan reached an amicable financial settlement with the university without litigation.

Case 4: *Jordan McNair was a 19-year-old offensive lineman at the University of Maryland. In May 2018, he suffered from heatstroke during practice and failed to receive adequate care, resulting in his death 15 days later. The investigation into McNair's death brought criticism to the University of Maryland and its athletic department, coaching staff, and personnel. Following an independent investigation into McNair's death, the programs' values, culture, and employees all came into question, as well as overarching concerns about the intensity of college athletic programs, especially football. This was not the first instance of problems with practices at the University of Maryland, or with other NCAA member institutions, related to the treatment, protection, and health of student-athletes. An independent firm, Walters, Inc., investigated and found that McNair was not removed from the field after showing symptoms,* *and it was not until 34 minutes had passed that he was taken to the training room. It took another 23 minutes after that for 911 to be called, alerting them to a medical emergency. After a total of 99 minutes had passed since McNair showed symptoms on the field, he left for the hospital in an ambulance, only after emergency medical services had arrived without directions, further delaying treatment. During the critical time that passed, the teams' trainers and coaches failed to accurately assess and treat McNair's symptoms. His temperature and vitals were not taken, he was not submersed in an ice bath, and proper treatment equipment was not readily available in the university's training room (Walters Inc., 2018).*

The family of Jordan McNair filed a notice of intent to sue the university for wrongful death, seeking up to $30 million in damages. However, in a compassionate and ethical statement to the media, rarely issued by higher education leaders or college football programs, the University of Maryland President Wallace Loh came forward after the Walters investigation and apologized to the McNair family, taking "legal and moral responsibility" for the death of Jordan McNair and promising change in the future. Legally, this admission of culpability and apology limited the university's ability to launch a successful defense or place blame elsewhere.

Case 4 is a tragic case that presented substantial legal exposure to the university, but revealed ethical leadership on the part of the university president. After initially placing involved athletic employees on administrative leave following the investigation into the incident, including Head Coach D. J. Durkin, Head Football Athletic Trainer Wes Robinson, and Assistant Athletic Director for Sports Performance Rick Court, the school made personnel changes in response to much pressure from the public. Ties were cut with Durkin after the university found that the McNair incident was not the only incident reflecting negligence or misconduct of the part of the football staff. The university has also announced that, in order to work towards a better program in the future, it is adopting and implementing many of the recommendations laid out in the Walters report, so that no student-athlete will suffer as Jordan McNair did. To many observers, President Loh's apology and acceptance of responsibility on the part of the university showed moral and ethical decision-making that reflected honesty, integrity, and compassion. In January 2021, the university also approved a $3.5 million financial settlement payment to the parents of Jordan McNair in resolution of the legal claims.

Closing Arguments

It is essential that sport managers understand the fundamental legal principles of tort law. Sport-related injuries to participants and spectators are often the result of negligence on the part of teams, schools, coaches, officials, facility managers, or facility owners. In these typical sport scenarios, there is a breach of a standard of care or a failure to act reasonably for the safety of others, resulting in injury that gives rise to claims based in negligence. In addition, there are other possible tort claims that occur on and off the field in sport, including gross negligence, product liability, and intentional torts such as battery and assault. The many case examples addressed in this chapter illustrate all these legal principles. They are instructive as to how tort claims arise and whether there is any legal defense to liability.

Risk management in sport organizations provides a necessary course of action to reduce the likelihood of injuries and protect organizations from civil liability. However, some managers and organizations approach ethical decision-making from purely a business perspective, prioritizing money and success over the well-being of those to whom they owe a duty of care. They also engage in cover-ups and rarely acknowledge moral responsibility for harm that might have been preventable. Such ethical failures may lead to severe financial and reputational consequences for sport organizations that choose to compromise health and safety.

Study Questions

1. What are the types of fact scenarios that give rise to claims of negligence in sport settings? Describe circumstances that might be a basis for gross negligence or intentional torts.
2. Do you think that the doctrine of assumption of risk should always prevail when participants compete in dangerous sports or recreational activities? Why/why not?
3. Discuss the ethical decision-making issues faced by an institution after a student-athlete is severely injured or dies during team practice or competition.
4. What specific risk management measures should college athletic departments consider and implement? Is it the same for all sports? Is there a greater duty owed by high school sport administrators to their student-athletes?

CHAPTER 3

Contract Law and Sport

Opening Statement

Contracts are prevalent at all levels of the sport industry and take many different forms. Sport managers must be familiar with the variety of circumstances where they will encounter contracts, such as game scheduling, event management, coaching (employment) hires, athlete endorsements, collective bargaining agreements, sport venue leases, season ticket sales, national letters of intent and scholarships, agent–athlete representation, and waivers and releases. A thorough understanding of the underlying principles of contract law is essential for those who have responsibility to manage or supervise any or all these areas. Ideally, these sport business relationships will be governed by a valid and enforceable contract, negotiated in good faith, and without ambiguity or legal deficiencies. However, as a practical matter, that does not always happen. Some contracts are poorly drafted or lack the requisite elements of contract formation. Some contracts are the product of unethical business practices or were induced by fraud. In some cases, a party to a contract simply fails or refuses to perform what was promised. For these reasons, contractual disputes are common in the sport industry and lawsuits frequently arise as a result.

Basic contract law includes the necessary elements to form a valid contract and the available legal remedies and damages if one or both parties are in breach of the contract terms. This chapter examines legal aspects of different types of sport contracts and, in the realm of intercollegiate athletics, the legal and ethical aspects of the "student-athlete" relationship created by the NCAA. That model is rooted in the principle of amateurism, which precludes college athletes from entering into certain contracts or receiving compensation for their services beyond the terms of their scholarship agreement.

Section I of this chapter addresses the fundamental legal principles of contract law. Specifically, it explains the required elements of contract formation, as well as the typical sport scenarios that give rise to legal claim of breach of contract. As a helpful guide for students, this section also includes sample

LEARNING OBJECTIVES

After reading this chapter, students will:

1. Understand the required elements of contract formation

2. Recognize the variety of sport-related contracts and how they are administered

3. Know common terms and provisions in coaching contracts

4. Understand the legal remedies and damages for breach of contract

5. Recognize typical fact scenarios that give rise to breach of contract cases in sport

6. Consider the ethical implications of NCAA Bylaws and amateurism rules

7. Understand the ethical issues surrounding the concept of student-athletes and academic fraud in college athletics

contract language found in typical sport contracts, with particular emphasis on coaching contracts at the intercollegiate level, which are the subject of much public interest and often end in legal disputes between departing coaches and their respective schools. There are many case decisions that illustrate these legal principles, and key cases will be identified and discussed in detail. Finally, this section explains how sport managers can implement best practices for contract drafting and contract administration within their school or sport organization.

Section II of this chapter addresses the ethical aspects of certain sport contracts, as well as the NCAA's amateurism model. As a legal matter, an athlete's national letter of intent in exchange for scholarship aid from their school constitutes an enforceable contract. Athletes who attend NCAA member institutions also agree to be bound by the NCAA Bylaws that govern their athletic participation including, among other things, academic eligibility and amateurism. Historically, the NCAA rules are based on the notion of student-athletes, a term coined by the NCAA to preserve amateurism and ensure that intercollegiate athletics has an educational mission. The amateurism rules are said to ensure that the athletes are students first, thus protecting education as the primary reason for attending a college or university. Ethically, however, many argue that college athletes are being exploited under this model. For example, is it ethical to limit the ability to earn money from an athlete's own name or likeness, or to preclude athletes from being paid for their athletic talents by agents or corporate sponsors? Also, there are ethical concerns with the imposition of academic standards as a condition of continued athletic participation in college. In some instances, this has been revealed as a sham, with widespread academic fraud at some institutions specifically designed to maintain athletic eligibility of their elite athletes. Those student-athletes have arguably been cheated of the education promised to them by their institution as part of their athletic scholarship agreement.

I. The Law

Contract Law: Fundamentals

Overview

Contracts are agreements, oral or written, that may be enforceable in court. The law of contracts involves a "promise, or set of promises, for breach of which the law gives a remedy" (Restatement [Second] of Contracts, §2, 1990). When parties enter a bilateral contract, one party promises to do something in exchange for something from the other party. For example, a promise to pay money in exchange for performance of services or an agreement to furnish equipment in exchange for payment of a designated price. Contracts are based in civil law and the typical remedy for breach of contract (i.e., when a party fails to perform what is promised) is the recovery of monetary damages.

Elements

This section examines the required elements to form a valid and enforceable contract. These elements are offer, acceptance, consideration, legality, and capacity.

Offer

An offer is made by one party (the "offeror") to another (the "offeree"), which creates a power of acceptance. It is a conditional promise to do or refrain from doing something in the future (Restatement [Second] of Contracts, §24, 1990). For example, John asks Mark to purchase his baseball glove for $100 if he responds in writing by midnight tonight. In that circumstance, John's detailed offer included the proposed sale of a specific item, for a specific price, and the time and method for acceptance. This created a power of acceptance in the offeree (Mark). This means that Mark has the ability to bind the offeror (John) to those terms.

Acceptance

Once an offer is made, the element of acceptance is necessary to satisfy the agreement of the parties. Acceptance must be communicated to the offeror in a positive manner, through words of conduct, and not by silence. Further, if the offer designates a particular method of acceptance (e.g., via text message or email), that must also be satisfied to achieve acceptance. In the hypothetical above, if Mark did not respond affirmatively to John until the next morning, or if he gave a verbal but not a written response, then Mark did not accept the offer as directed by the offeror. Also, if Mark replied on time but changed the price from $100 to $50, then there was not a valid acceptance. Under those circumstances, Mark conveyed a counteroffer to John instead of an acceptance. If a valid offer is extended and a timely acceptance is communicated in the manner requested, then the parties have achieved "mutual assent" or a "meeting of the minds." The contract is not yet fully enforceable, however, until it is demonstrated that the remaining elements are satisfied.

Consideration

After mutual assent is established, there must be consideration before a contract can be legally enforceable. Consideration is an exchange of value between the parties, whereby each party agrees to give some value or benefit to the other as part of the contract. Each party must receive something in return, although not necessarily of equal value. For example, Susan pays Kathy $1,000 in return for piano lessons. Or Team ABC promises to pay Venue X a monthly fee of $5,000 in exchange for the use of their facility. In contrast, gifts cannot serve as consideration because the giving party did not receive something in return. Similarly, rewards for past services are not a basis for consideration because the party who paid the reward did not receive something in exchange at the time of the reward payment.

Legality

The element of legality must be established even if the offer, acceptance, and consideration are satisfied. Legality means that the subject matter of the contract, or the underlying transaction itself, is legal. If a contract is based upon an illegal act or transaction, it is not enforceable. In the examples above, all the underlying acts or transactions (baseball equipment, piano lessons, facility rental) constitute legal acts or activities, and the legality element is thus satisfied. On the other hand, legality will not be met if the underlying transaction was for sports betting or for the sale of certain drugs, in jurisdictions where such activities were illegal. Again, legality examines whether the subject matter of the contract (not the contract itself) is a legal act or transaction.

Capacity

The final element of contract formation is capacity. Under the law, certain groups of people lack the mental competence or ability to enter into a binding contract. This could include persons of diminished mental capacity, persons under the influence of drugs or alcohol, and those under the legal age in a particular jurisdiction. Regarding age, there are still many examples of minors who are party to a sport contract. Under applicable law, a contract between a minor and an adult may be voided by the minor but is still enforceable against the adult. Also, in some cases, the contract with a minor may be binding upon the minor if the minor's parents or guardians have agreed on behalf of the minor.

Contract Interpretation and Breach

Contract disputes commonly arise when the contract terms or language is ambiguous, or when one or both parties fail to meet their obligations or promises.

Contract Interpretation

Contract interpretation is when a court determines the meaning of the contract terms. The question of whether a contract is clear is a question of law for the court to decide. Courts must interpret the contract as written and then give effect to the mutual intention of the parties at the time of contracting. Written contracts also typically contain what is called an "integration clause." In contract law, an integration clause is used to declare that the written contract is the complete and final agreement between the parties. This means that the written terms supersede any prior negotiations or agreements, oral or written, between the parties. If there is a valid integration clause, a court may not consider other evidence related to the contract terms or conditions that were not included in the written agreement.

Breach of Contract

A breach of contract occurs when a party does not perform as promised or fails to meet its obligations under a contract. In such circumstances, the non-breaching party has certain rights under the principles of contract law. They can commence a legal action (lawsuit) for breach of contract and request that the court impose certain remedies, including monetary damages, to compensate the non-breaching party for their losses. A basic example of breach of contract is as follows: Dan and Adam enter into a contract for the sale of certain sports equipment. Dan agrees to deliver 100 baseball bats to Adam, within 7 days, for a total price of $2,000. Adam timely pays the full amount to Dan; however, Dan fails to timely provide the baseball bats. In that example, Dan committed a breach of contract as he did not perform as promised. Because Dan failed to satisfy his obligations under the material terms of the contract, Adam has a potential claim for breach of contract.

Remedies and Damages for Breach

After a breach occurs, the non-breaching party may seek certain remedies and damages from the court. Typically, this involves recovery of monetary damages to compensate the non-breaching party for their losses. Monetary damages are awarded in such cases to make the non-breaching party "whole" or to put them in the position they would have been in had the contract been performed as agreed. There are different ways to quantify appropriate monetary damages in a breach of contract case, and those are identified below. In rare cases, there is a potential remedy for breach of contract called "specific performance," which is also discussed below. Specific performance applies in circumstances where monetary compensation is deemed inadequate.

Compensatory Damages

One form of monetary damages is known as compensatory damages. These are determined based on the amount of money necessary to compensate the non-breaching party for their monetary loss. In the breach of contract example above, Adam should recover $2,000 in compensatory damages, based on Dan's breach. That is the amount Adam paid to Dan for baseball bats that Dan failed to timely furnish as promised.

Consequential Damages

Consequential damages are a form of monetary damages that are measured by the indirect monetary losses that flowed from the breach. In the example above, suppose that Adam purchased the baseball bats from Dan for use at his summer baseball camp that was scheduled to start in 7 days. Also suppose that 100 campers then cancelled their registration and demanded refunds when Adam's camp did not have essential equipment for baseball instruction. Dan's failure to timely provide the baseball bats in those circumstances resulted in not only compensatory losses of $2,000, but also consequential damages based on the refunds that were indirectly caused by Dan's breach. Adam would be entitled to both compensatory and consequential damages that he can prove in court.

Liquidated Damages

In some cases, the contracting parties decide in advance on the specific monetary damages to be awarded in the event of breach by either party. These are known as liquidated damages. Liquidated damages are agreed up front and are memorialized in the written contract. In a breach of contract lawsuit, liquidated damages make it easy for the court to determine how much must be paid by the breaching party, as it is stated in the contract itself. Liquidated damage provisions are common in several types of sport contracts, including coaching contracts (stating the amounts owed at the time of termination) and game contracts (specifying a "forfeit fee" if one team fails to play the game as promised). A well-known case involving reciprocal liquidated damages in a college coaching contract is noted later in this chapter under Coaching Contracts (*Vanderbilt University v. DiNardo*, 1999).

> **Case Hypothetical: Monetary Damages Analysis**
>
> In this hypothetical case, Dave is an elite runner who signs an endorsement contract with shoe manufacturer EKIN. Dave agrees to exclusively wear EKIN shoes for 5 years and make personal appearances at EKIN events. EKIN agrees to pay Dave a $1 million signing bonus, and $2 million/year for each year of the contract. As part of the contract, EKIN also expends $500,000 to design the "Dave" shoe and $250,000 in marketing and advertising before paying Dave the signing bonus. EKIN projects they will make $20 million in profits over the 5-year term of the contract. After 1 year, however, Dave decides he can get a better offer from SCISA shoes and informs EKIN that he cannot fulfill the remaining 4 years.

Based on the above facts, Dave committed a material breach of contract by leaving EKIN, and EKIN did not receive what they bargained for. EKIN will seek **compensatory damages**, which would include the return of the signing bonus, first-year payment to Dave, and money for design and advertising spent in reliance on the contract. EKIN might also seek **consequential damages** in the form of the estimated lost profits that indirectly flowed from Dave's breach. The lost profits (consequential) are more speculative and will require sufficient proof from experts at trial. There were no **liquidated damages** stated in the above hypothetical. However, if Dave and EKIN had agreed upon specific damages in the event of a breach, then the court would award those liquidated damages to EKIN as their exclusive remedy.

Specific Performance

Some contract cases involve unique subject matter. In such cases, monetary damages might be inadequate to fully compensate the non-breaching party for their losses. A possible legal remedy in those cases is called specific performance. This requires the breaching party to perform the contract as promised. This does not apply to employment contracts, as it is unconstitutional to force an individual to perform work or labor. Specific performance might apply to the sale of a parcel of land (considered unique) or the sale of World Series tickets (special event), where monetary damages are insufficient to compensate the losses. In those examples, if a breach of contract occurred, the court might order the breaching party to convey the parcel of land as promised, or deliver the World Series tickets as agreed, instead of awarding monetary compensation. Similar facts gave rise to specific performance in a case filed by a group of Louisiana State University football fans against the University of Illinois. In that case, the fans did not receive tickets they had duly purchased to a prestigious college bowl game. After the court found that the defendant had breached the contract, it determined that specific performance was the appropriate remedy in lieu of monetary damages. The defendant was ordered to furnish the plaintiffs with the tickets that were promised in the sale (*Levert v. University of Illinois at Urbana/Champaign through the Board of Trustees*, 2003).

Contract Administration: Best Practices for Management

There are best practices that sport managers should follow when involved in drafting, negotiating, and administering contracts. First, although verbal contracts may be enforceable, it is best to ensure that contracts are in writing and drafted by competent and qualified personnel. Second, if you are engaged in contract negotiations, you should do so in good faith and with a thorough understanding of what is agreed and required. Third, note all critical deadlines, and if the contract calls for performance by third parties, take all necessary steps to see that is accomplished. Fourth, maintain confidentiality when required and share contract terms only with those in your organization who have a "need to know." Finally, from a management perspective, it is essential to educate staff and key personnel on potential consequences in the event of a breach.

Sample Sport Contracts and Key Provisions

There are many different types of contracts utilized in the sport industry. Some of the most common types are identified below, including the key terms and conditions typically included in the respective contracts. Note that there is no single template that covers each type of contract; the final format and provisions are dependent upon what was negotiated between the parties and drafting consistent language, preferably with assistance of legal counsel. These include collective bargaining agreements used by professional sport leagues, game contracts in high school sports, endorsement contracts, leases for sport venues, season ticket contracts, agent–athlete representation contracts, national letters of intent and scholarships in intercollegiate athletics, and participation waivers and releases. A separate section that follows is devoted to coaching contracts and the key aspects that apply to employment contract language and available remedies upon termination.

Collective Bargaining Agreements

A collective bargaining agreement (CBA) is a type of sport contract used by professional sport leagues. It is a comprehensive contract that contains the negotiated terms and conditions of employment between player unions and team owners. CBAs are typically hundreds of pages in length and cover the entire relationship between a players' association (union) and the owners (management) over a period of years. The four major professional sport leagues in the United States (NFL, MLB, NBA, NHL) are each governed by a CBA.

To illustrate the comprehensive nature of a professional sport league CBA, it is helpful to examine the applicable table of contents. The current NBA Collective Bargaining Agreement is publicly available online on the players association (NBPA) website: https://nbpa.com/cba. A cursory review shows that it is nearly 600 pages long (including multiple exhibits) and is effective for 7 years, during the period July 1, 2017, through June 30, 2024. It covers areas including, without limitation, the player draft, health and wellness, salary cap, All-Star Game, grievance and arbitration procedures, and anti-drug program. It also includes, as Exhibit A, the required standard form of the NBA Uniform Player Contract. That is a separate contract between individual players and their teams, to reflect each athlete's employment by a particular team as a professional basketball player.

Game Contract

School athletic directors and administrators at all levels are accustomed to the use of game contracts when scheduling and confirming sport competitions between opposing teams. A game contract should outline the specifics of the game time, location, officials, concessions, tickets, payment of expenses and revenues, and so on. Depending upon the nature and scale of the game or event, there might also be consideration of television rights, sponsorship opportunities, appearance money, and/or penalty fees in the event of forfeit or cancellation. The document below is a sample high school football game contract utilized by the University Interscholastic League in Texas. It reveals the scope of issues that must be addressed, even at the high school level, to schedule and facilitate sport competition.

University Interscholastic League
Football Game Contract

THIS AGREEMENT, entered into this _____ day of _____, 20__, by and between _____, _____(title), _____(home town), High School, hereinafter designated as the part of the first part, and _____, _____, of _____(visiting team), High School, hereinafter designated as the party of the second part, stipulates as follows:

1. The said parties mutually agree to cause the _____ teams of the high school of which they are respectively officials to meet in the city of _____ on the _____ day of _____, 20_____, and then and there engage in a game of _____, said game to start at or about _____ o'clock, p.m.

2. The above mentioned game of _____ shall be conducted under the University Interscholastic League rules and regulations in force at the time of the game, with the provisions of which rules and regulations each of the signers hereto declares himself to be familiar, and any provision of this contract contravening any rule of the League shall invalidate the whole contract.

3. The part of the first part agrees to provide a playing field or court for said game, to collect admission fees and to make a business settlement under the terms of this contract within a reasonable time after the conclusion of said game.

4. The party of the first part agrees to pay the part of the second part:
    a. the sum of $_____ for playing said game or, in lieu thereof, at the option of the party of the second part,
    b. actual traveling expenses of a party to the number of _____, said expenses to consist of cost of transportation of the party to the number of _____, from _____, Texas, to_____, Texas, and reasonable hotel expenses, together with one-half of the net gate receipts of said game. It is agreed that the above mentioned traveling expenses shall be considered as an expense of the game in computing the net gate receipts.

5. Both parties agree that in case they fail mutually to agree upon officials for said above mentioned game at least 7 days prior to the time set for the game, the Athletic Director of the Interscholastic League shall have authority to appoint the officials necessary for the proper conduct of said game.

6. In case either party fails to produce his team and play the said game on said date and at said place, or breaches any clause of this agreement, the party so in fault agrees to pay to the party not in fault the sum of $_____ as a forfeit within one week of the date on which said breach of contract shall occur, together with all expenses incurred in pursuance of this contract by the team which is not at fault, such payment to be conclusive of further damages, except in case of breach of Clause Number 4 above.

University Interscholastic League, "University Interscholastic League Football Game Contract." Copyright © by UIL Texas.

7. In case either the _____ High School or the _____ High School shall be suspended in the sport of _____ from the Interscholastic League, this agreement shall become null and void.

8. Both parties agree to the (1) radio broadcast; (2) telecast; or (3) tape delay of the contest, with the understanding that any income from said broadcast/telecast shall be considered in the gross receipts.

Signed in duplicate:

_____

Superintendent/Principal

_____ High School

_____

Superintendent/Principal

_____ High School

(Duplicate as needed)   (Revised 1-2000)

Source: https://www.uiltexas.org/football/forms

Facility Lease Agreements

A lease is a type of contract entered into between a property owner ("lessor") and a party ("lessee") who uses the property for a specific price (rent) and time. Leases are often identified in connection with residential apartments or commercial property office rentals. In sport, it is common to see lease agreements between a facility owner and a team or sport organization that will use the facility for competition. Under a typical sport lease agreement, the lessee pays periodic rent in exchange for the use of the facility. In professional sports, lease agreements may become lengthy and complex, as the lessor may be one or more public entities, and the lease must address issues such as exclusive use, non-relocation, funding, construction, development, maintenance, and operations. In exchange for the facility usage, professional sport teams will pay substantial annual rental payments to the lessor(s).

Endorsement Contracts

Endorsement contracts between athletes and sponsors are common in professional sport. Athlete endorsements have significant commercial value for corporations within the sport industry and beyond. A typical endorsement contract gives the corporate sponsor the right to use an athlete's name, image, and likeness in connection with their marketing and advertising. The amount of money paid to athletes for exclusive endorsement agreements is very substantial with well-known sports figures. Highly compensated athletes in many sports often receive endorsement income that exceeds their actual salary in a team sport or their competitive earnings in individual sports like tennis and golf. That has consistently been the case for popular and charismatic athletes such as LeBron James, Tiger Woods, Roger Federer, and Maria Sharapova.

Sample language in an endorsement contract would include a specific definition of "endorsement" (name, image, etc.), the scope of products to be worn or endorsed, exclusivity, and the specific term (length) of the agreement.

Agent Representation

Agents are common in professional sport. They represent athletes in contract negotiations, not only with teams, but also with potential endorsers. Agency law involves the relationship between a principal and an agent, where the agent is authorized to act on behalf of the principal. Agents must act in good faith for the benefit of the principal, exercise reasonable care and skill to provide information to the principal, and only to the scope and extent expressly authorized. This is also known as a fiduciary duty that an agent owes to the principal. The principal, in turn, owes a duty of fair compensation to the agent. In athlete-agent representation, the athlete is the principal. In exchange for such services, the athlete typically pays compensation to the agent in the form of fixed fees or agreed percentages of income. An agent representation agreement is an important type of sport contract that must be carefully drafted and fully understood prior to signing.

Historically, sport agents were not regulated by federal or state law. Unfortunately, as the representation of athletes became more competitive and lucrative, many unscrupulous individuals were involved in scamming athletes for money or engaging in double-dealing and other conflicts of interest. These scandals also permeated college sports, and while the NCAA Bylaws prohibited signing with agents as a violation of amateurism rules, many college stars were enticed to sign early in exchange for promised money to themselves or their families. In 2000, a model state law was created, for individual states to adopt, which provided for uniformity in registration and certification of athlete agents. This was known as the Uniform Athlete Agents Act (UAAA). Nearly all states have enacted the UAAA, for example, the state of North Carolina referenced in the Williamson case discussed below, N.C. Gen. Stat. §§78C-85-78C-105 (2014). Various efforts for federal legislation proved unsuccessful until the passage of the Sports Agent Responsibility and Trust Act (SPARTA) in 2004, which protects student-athletes and their schools from improper agent relationships and interference (15 U.S.C. §§ 7801-7807).

Case Notes: *Williamson v. Prime Sports Marketing, LLC*

Zion Williamson was a star basketball player for Duke University prior to entering the NBA. During his freshman season in 2018–19, he was projected as a number one draft pick, expected to leave college for the pros after one year. He declared for the NBA draft in April 2019, at which time he also signed a "marketing agent agreement" with sports agent Gina Ford and her company Prime Sports Marketing (PSM). Williamson later signed with another agency and sued in North Carolina to void his contract with PSM based on alleged violation of state unfair trade practices law, and specifically a violation of the North Carolina Uniform Athlete Agents Act (NCUAAA). Ford and her company countersued Williamson in the state of Florida, seeking $100 million in damages, which was the alleged value of her commissions had the contract been fulfilled. The NCUAAA claims raised by Williamson were based upon the fact that Ford did not hold a certificate of agency registration in North Carolina and that the marketing agent agreement did not include the required statutory language in that the athlete would lose their eligibility to compete in their sport in college upon signing. In January 2021, the North

Carolina court ruled that Williamson's contract with his former agent Gina Ford and her company Prime Sports Marketing, LLC, is void because they did not follow NCUAAA. The court rejected the defense arguments that the former Duke University player had violated NCAA eligibility rules.

National Letter of Intent and Scholarships

A National Letter of Intent (NLI) is a part of the contractual relationship between an athlete and their school. In exchange for the NLI, the school provides the athletic scholarship, which binds them to provide the athlete financial aid and the opportunity to participate in their sport. In some circumstances, an NLI is potentially unenforceable, for example, if the athlete is ineligible under NCAA rules, or if the school determines that the athlete is not academically admissible. Under the current NCAA Bylaws, multiyear scholarships are permissible, but may not exceed 5 years (*NCAA Bylaw* 15.3.3.1, as amended).

The acceptance of a scholarship requires the athlete to maintain certain grade levels and to perform as an athlete for a school in return for tuition, books, and certain other educational expenses. This constitutes an enforceable bilateral contract (*Taylor v. Wake Forest University*, 1972). There have been many legal efforts to treat scholarship athletes as employees instead of student-athletes. The argument advanced in support of this idea is that college athletes, particularly those in Division I football and men's basketball, are "quasi-professionals," working long hours under the direction and supervision of their coaches, and that schools benefit financially from their services. In that sense, it is argued that the relationship is more akin to that of a business with employees. Significantly, if an employment relationship were legally recognized, this would lead to certain rights and responsibilities, such as the unionization of college athletes under federal labor laws, worker's compensation benefits for injured athletes, minimum wage and hours, and tax liability on scholarship moneys. It would also contravene NCAA principles of amateurism and the educational mission of college athletics. To date, the cases alleging employment-based claims on behalf of student-athletes have been unsuccessful.

The following are typical provisions contained in an NLI. Sample (1) (a) – (e) sets forth when an NLI may be declared null and void. Sample (2) relates to the recruiting ban that is effective upon signing (http://www.nationalletter.org/nliProvisions/index.html).

> **Sample (1): This NLI shall be declared null and void if any of the following occur.**
>
> a. **Admissions Requirement.** This NLI shall be declared null and void if the institution named in this document notifies me in writing that I have been denied admission or, by the opening day of classes in the fall, has failed to provide me with written notice of admission, provided I have submitted a complete admission application. It is my obligation to provide, by request, my academic records and an application for admission to the signing institution. If I fail to submit the necessary academic credentials and/or application to determine an admission decision prior to September 1, the NLI office per its review with the institution will determine the status of the NLI.
>
> If I am eligible for admission, but the institution named in this document defers my admission to a subsequent term, the NLI will be declared null and void; however, this NLI remains binding if I defer my admission.

b. **Eligibility Requirements.** This NLI shall be declared null and void if, by the opening day of classes in the fall, I have not met NCAA initial eligibility requirements; NCAA, conference, or institution's requirements for athletics financial aid; or two-year college transfer requirements, provided I have submitted all necessary documents for eligibility determination.

[...]

c. **One-Year Absence.**
d. **Discontinued Sport.**
e. **Recruiting Rules Violation.**

Sample (2): Recruiting Ban After Signing

I understand all participating conferences and institutions are obligated to respect my signing and shall cease contact with me and my family members after my signing this NLI, which includes me and my family members not initiating contact with athletic staffs at other institutions. Any contact in excess of an exchange of a greeting is not permitted regardless of the conversation. The conversation does not have to result in recruiting discussion for a recruiting ban violation to occur. I shall notify any coach who contacts me that I have signed an NLI. Once I enroll in the institution named in this document, the NLI Recruiting Ban is no longer in effect and I shall be governed by applicable NCAA Bylaws.

NIL Agreements

Recently enacted state laws across the country have led to opportunities for college athletes to earn substantial income by monetizing their names, images, and likenesses (NILs) through contractual agreements with third parties. Examples of such agreements include product endorsements, appearances for local businesses, and provision of lessons or clinics for developing athletes. In response to these laws and considerable public pressure, the NCAA revised its rules that previously barred such agreements and related compensation for college athletes as violative of NCAA amateurism principles.

Participation Waivers and Releases

Waivers and releases are commonly used by sport organizations to shield themselves from liability for injuries suffered by participants. These are a type of sport contract that also incorporates tort principles addressed in the previous chapter. It is premised on the idea that a contract may be entered into to absolve a party of legal liability. However, such releases are subjected to scrutiny, and many states are reluctant to enforce them as violative of public policy because it involves the relinquishment of legal rights. To be enforceable, most courts have ruled that waivers and releases must be carefully drafted to ensure that they (a) are conspicuous (not fine print), (b) are unambiguous (clear and concise), (c) are detailed and specific, and (d) only extend to negligence (cannot release claims for gross negligence or intentional misconduct). This is also the rare type of sport contract where a court will examine the fairness of the agreement to determine its enforceability. A court might void a waiver and release that was the product of unequal bargaining power, was signed under duress, is overly broad, or involves a minor child participant.

The document below is a clearly drafted, detailed, and specific waiver and release used by a sport organization whose participants engage in the sport of "cold-plunging." Because the sport involves serious risks, including death, to its participants, the waiver and release agreement carefully identifies the risks and requires multiple acknowledgments by the participant that they are knowingly and willfully engaging in this dangerous activity. In the event the participant does incur harm or injury while participating in cold-plunging, this waiver and release could be effective to protect the organizers from tort liability. This document also includes a photo release form that grants permission for the organization to use a participant's photo or likeness and releases the organization from a participant's expectation of confidentiality or compensation for such use.

Lakeview Polar Bear Club
Waiver and Release Agreement
PLEASE READ CAREFULLY BEFORE SIGNING.
THIS IS A RELEASE OF LIABILITY AND WAIVER OF CERTAIN LEGAL RIGHTS.

In consideration of my being permitted to participate in the Lakeview Polar Bear Club Charity Fundraiser Lake Plunge (hereafter referred to as "the Event"), I agree to the following waiver and release:

I acknowledge that jumping into cold water, standing and walking upon ice, walking and lingering in the snow in the vicinity of the Event, lingering near and among the crowd gathered for the Event, and traveling to and from the Event and its various attractions have inherent risks, hazards and dangers. I understand that these risks, hazards and dangers include without limitation:

(1) risks arising from exposure to large and sudden changes in environmental temperatures that can lead to loss of consciousness, hypothermia, heart attacks, and other life-threatening conditions;
(2) risks involved in standing and moving about on frozen lakes and reservoirs and on snowy, icy, or irregular terrain;
(3) such other risks, hazards, and dangers that are inherent to the sport of cold plunging and being out of doors during winter.

please initial: _____

I am voluntarily participating in the Event with full knowledge of the inherent risks, hazards, and dangers involved and hereby assume and accept any and all risks of injury, paralysis, or death, and agree to abide by all Lakeview Polar Bear Club rules, regulations, and guidelines.

please initial: _____

I, for myself, my heirs, successors, executors, and superiors, hereby knowingly and intentionally waive and release, indemnify, and hold harmless the Lakeview Polar Bear Club or any of their officers, agents, affiliates, employees, contractors, sponsors, or volunteers, as well as the Chicago Park District, and members of the Chicago Park District Board of Commissioners, and the officers, agents, and employees of the Chicago Park District, individually and collectively, from and against any and all claims, actions, causes of action, liabilities, suits, expenses (including reasonable attorney's fees) and negligence of any kind or nature, whether foreseen or unforeseen,

Lakeview Polar Bear Club, "Lakeview Polar Bear Club Waiver and Release Agreement." Copyright © by Lakeview Polar Bear Club.

arising directly or indirectly out of any damage, loss, injury, paralysis, or death to me or my property as a result of participation in the Event, whether such damage, loss, injury, paralysis, or death results from the negligence or other acts however caused by or contributed to by the Lakeview Polar Bear Club and all related entities named above, or from some other cause. I, for myself, my heirs, my successors, executors, and superiors, further agree not to sue Lakeview Polar Bear Club, their officers, agents, affiliates, employees, contractors, sponsors, or volunteers, as well as the Chicago Park District, and members of the Chicago Park District Board of Commissioners, and the officers, agents, and employees of the Chicago Park District, individually and collectively, as a result of any injury, paralysis or death suffered in connection with my participation in the Event. I attest that I am of the age of 18 years or older.

The Lakeview Polar Bear Club reserves the right to remove me from the water, at any time, for any reasonable cause.

please initial: _____

I have carefully read, clearly understand, and voluntarily sign this waiver and release agreement.

_____
Signature   Date   City   State   Zip

_____   _____
Print Name   Phone

_____   _____
Mailing Address   Email Address

If under 18 years of age, parent or guardian must sign the following Indemnification

In consideration for the above minor being permitted to participate in the Event, I agree to the following waiver, release and indemnification:

The undersigned parent and guardian of the above minor, for himself/herself and on behalf of said minor hereby joins in the foregoing waiver and release and hereby stipulates and agrees to save and hold harmless, indemnify, and forever defend the Lakeview Polar Bear Club and any of their officers, agents, affiliates, employees, contractors, sponsors, or volunteers, from and against any and all claims, actions, demands, expenses liabilities (including reasonable attorney's fees) and negligence made or brought by said minor or by anyone on behalf of said minor, as a result of said minor's participation in the Event. I, for myself and on behalf of said minor, further agree not to sue the Lakeview Polar Bear Club or any of their officers, agents, affiliates, employees, contractors, or volunteers, as a result of any injury, paralysis or death that said minor suffers in connection with participation in the Event.

_____   _____   _____
Signature of Parent or Guardian of Minor   Date   Print Name of Minor

_____   _____   _____
Print Name of Parent or Guardian   Witness   Date

Lakeview Polar Bear Club
Waiver and Release Agreement
STANDARD PHOTO RELEASE FORM

I hereby give my consent for Lakeview Polar Bear Club to use my photograph and likeness in any Lakeview Polar Bear Club or sponsor's hard copy and/or electronic publications, including Web sites. I release them from any expectation of confidentiality or compensation for myself and any undersigned minor children and attest that I am the parent or legal guardian of the children listed below.

Signature: _____ Date: _____

Names and Ages of Minor Children:

Name: _____ Age: _____

Name: _____ Age: _____

Name: _____ Age: _____

Source: Lakeview Polar Bear Club

Coaching Contracts

Coaching contracts with universities or professional sport teams raise special concerns. Compensation packages for coaches are often incredibly complex, with substantial annual salaries, perquisites, and benefits. It is not unusual that a college football or basketball coach at a public university is the highest-paid public employee in that entire state. Historically, coaching contracts were often based on mere handshakes or verbal agreements. But they have evolved in recent years into negotiated and lengthy agreements with many essential terms and conditions. The spotlight generally focuses on the salary of the coach, but the other terms of the contract are equally important. With growing concerns over winning games, student-athlete misconduct, and rules compliance with governing bodies, the coaching contract is significant not only in the narrow employment context but also has potential financial and competitive implications for teams, athletic programs, universities, and sponsors.

Coaching contracts are a specific type of employment agreement, as a coach is hired as an employee of an organization to perform certain duties in exchange for salary and other forms of compensation. Coaching contracts can be lengthy and complicated, so it is important to first understand and identify the material terms of the agreement. A material term is one related to significant issues, such as payment, subject matter, performance, bonuses, and termination. Several other terms are addressed in a coaching contract that are equally important to review.

The material terms to know are

- term
- salary (base and supplemental)
- bonuses
- termination (for cause, without cause)
- liquidated damages and buyouts

Additional terms to be familiar with are

- duties
- perquisites
- reassignment
- mitigation

Another important document to know is called a Memorandum of Understanding (MOU), also referred to as an offer letter. Many high-level coaching contracts are preceded by an MOU. This document outlines and defines the material terms of an agreement. Generally, this is a short letter that serves as the underlying basis for the subsequent long-form contract. In many cases, due to the urgency and quick hiring process for coaching positions, the MOU dictates the terms of the agreement until the long-form contract is fully executed. Sample language from an MOU regarding a head coach position at a university is set forth below.

January 2, 2019

Dana Holgorsen
Via Email

RE: Memorandum of Understanding

Dear Dana:

It is with great pleasure I offer you the position of Head Coach of the Intercollegiate Football team ("Coaching Position") at the University of Houston ("University"), beginning on January 1, 2019 and ending on December 31, 2023. The Coaching Position reports to me, in my role as Vice President for Intercollegiate Athletics. This binding Memorandum of Understanding, which presents the material terms of our offer, will be expanded and incorporated into a mutually agreed upon employment contract with the University for execution at the earliest possible date. Said employment contract will be for a period of five (5) years at mutually agreed upon terms and conditions.

Dana Holgorsen/University of Houston MOU
Source: https://gocoogs.com/dana-holgorsens-mou/

In other coaching contract negotiations, a Term Sheet might be utilized by the parties. A Term Sheet is typically written informally, sometimes in bullet points, to outline the material terms of the agreement. This is non-binding until the formal execution of a contract that conforms to the listed terms and conditions. A sample Term Sheet for the hiring of a head coach for women's basketball at a university is set forth below.

Term Sheet Between Louisiana State University and Kimberly Mulkey

Position: Head Coach for Women's Basketball at LSU

Reporting: Coach shall report directly to Scott Woodward, Athletics Director

Term: Effective no later than June 1, 2021 and ending June 30, 2029

Compensation: (annual rates; pro-rated for partial years)

- Base Salary: $ 400,000
- Supplemental Compensation:

Through June 30, 2022:	$2,045,000
July 1, 2022 through June 30, 2023:	$2,120,000
July 1, 2023 through June 30, 2024:	$2,195,000
July 1, 2024 through June 30, 2025:	$2,300,000
July 1, 2025 through June 30, 2026:	$2,345,000
July 1, 2026 through June 30, 2027:	$2,647,000
July 1, 2027 through June 30, 2028:	$2,727,000
July 1, 2028 through June 30, 2029:	$2,902,000

- Additional Sponsor-Related Compensation: $ 60,000

Incentives:[1]
- Southeastern Conference:
    - SEC Regular Season Champion — $ 65,000 AND
    - SEC Tournament Championship — $ 35,000
- NCAA Tournament Appearance:
    - First Round — $ 28,000 AND
    - Round of 32 — $ 30,000 AND
    - Sweet 16 — $ 33,000[2] AND
    - Elite 8 — $ 38,000 AND
    - Final Four — $ 50,000[3] AND
    - National Championship Game — $ 75,000[4] AND
    - NCAA Tournament Champion — $150,000
- Coach of the Year:
    - Southeastern Conference Coach of the Year — $ 10,000
    - National Coach of the Year — $ 15,000

- Top 25 Finish:
  - Final Ranking 11-25 $ 25,000 Or

[1] Additional performance-based incentives to be negotiated.
[2] Plus additional $5,000 sponsor-related incentive bonus payable if team does not advance to the Final Four or
[3] Plus additional $15,000 sponsor-related incentive bonus payable if the team does not advance to National Championship or
[4] Plus additional $30,000 sponsor-related incentive bonus.

Term Sheet – Kimberly Mulkey
Page 1 of 2
Kimberly Mulkey/LSU Term Sheet, p. 1 of 2
Source: https://www.theadvocate.com/baton_rouge/sports/lsu/article_45066fec-a840-11eb-994b-57b1c1e3cf93.html

Material Terms in Coaching Contracts

Term

Coaching contracts have a beginning date and an end date. The "term" of the contract is the defined length of time the contract will be in full force and effect. The end date may be amended to extend the term. This would be done by executing either a new contract or an addendum to the original contract. It is important to include specific dates when defining the term of the agreement.

Salary

Compensation needs to be agreed upon as a material term of any coaching agreement. Some coaches will receive an annual salary that is consistent throughout the term, while others may have an annual escalating salary. Compensation will generally be listed as either "base salary" or "supplemental salary" (non-salary compensation). The base salary is the standard rate of pay, while the supplemental salary is awarded for a variety of reasons. Generally, this supplemental salary or additional compensation constitutes most of the payment to the highest paid coaches.

> (a) <u>Base Salary.</u> As compensation for the services performed under this Agreement, the Head Coach shall be paid a base salary ("Base Salary") of $500,000 per Contract Year.
>
> (b) The Base Salary provided for above shall be paid to the Head Coach in accordance with the University's normal payroll procedures.
>
> (c) <u>Additional Compensation.</u> The Head Coach will receive additional compensation at the annual rate of $4,500,000, paid in equal monthly installments, as compensation for his television, radio, internet, public relations, promotional activities, personal appearances in connection with his duties under this Agreement, support of the University's shoe and apparel sponsorships, and other activities as part of his duties and responsibilities as the Head Coach ("Additional Compensation").

Jim Harbaugh/University of Michigan Employment Agreement
Source: http://media.mlive.com/wolverines_impact/other/Harbaugh%20employment%20agrmt.pdf

Deferred compensation can be included as part of the salary as well. Many coaches use attorneys and financial advisors to structure deferred compensation payments in a tax-efficient manner.

> 1. Deferred Compensation
> The parties have negotiated in good faith a deferred compensation arrangement for you, the terms of which are set forth in the 457(f) Deferred Compensation Agreement (the "Deferred Compensation Agreement") between you and the University. The basic terms of the Deferred Compensation Agreement, as covered in greater detail in the Deferred Compensation Agreement, are as set forth herein. The University has established a bookkeeping record on your behalf, referred to as the "Deferred Compensation Account," for the sole purpose of measuring your benefit under the Deferred Compensation Agreement. As of each July 1 (beginning July 1, 2009 and ending July 1, 2015), so long as you remain employed as the University's Head Men's Basketball Coach, the University shall credit this Deferred Compensation Account with $60,000.
>
> *Shaka Smart/Virginia Commonwealth University Employment Agreement*
> *Source: https://static.texastribune.org/media/documents/Smart_Contract_2013.pdf*

Bonuses

The emphasis on winning is reflected in the bonus structure of coaching contracts. In addition to incentives for team and coaching success, there may be bonuses for college coaches related to academic performance of their student-athletes. Each bonus has a specifically designated amount. Depending on the sport, the amount and accomplishment of the bonuses will vary, but many college coaching contracts have bonuses relating to conference and NCAA championships, coach of the year awards, and academic progress rate (APR). Bonus money is a material term that is negotiated and varies by sport and institution. The amount may be determined by exact amount or a percentage of the salary.

> *(Bonuses for head coach, men's basketball)*
>
> **Section 2.3.1. SEC Achievements.** Either or both of the following per Contract Year:
>
> | | |
> |---|---|
> | a. Winning the SEC Regular Season Championship (solo or shared) (as determined by the SEC) | $400,000 |
> | b. Winning the SEC Tournament Championship | $200,000 |
>
> **Section 2.3.1. NCAA Achievement.** A maximum of one (1) of the following per Contract Year (payment based on highest goa1 achieved in this subsection):
>
> | | |
> |---|---|
> | a. Winning the NCAA Championship | $1,500,000 |
> | b. Appearing in the NCAA Championship Game | $1,200.000 |
> | c. Appearing in the Final Four | $1,000,000 |
> | d. Appearing in the Elite Eight | $800,000 |
> | e. Appearing in the Sweet Sixteen | $600,000 |
> | f. Appearing in the Round of 32 | $400,000 |
> | g. Appearing in the NCAA Tournament | $200,000 |

Section 2.3.3. Coach of the Year Achievements. Either or both of the following per Contract Year:
   a. National Coach of the Year (AP, Naismith, or USBWA)
     (solo or shared) $250,000
   b. AP SEC Coach of the Year (solo or shared) $150,000

Section 2.3.4. National Ranking Achievement. A maximum of one (1) of the following per Contract Year (payment based on highest goal achieved in this subsection):
   a. Top-5 Ranking in final Associated Press poll $400,000
   b. Top-10 Ranking in final Associated Press poll $200,000
   c. Top-25 Ranking in final Associated Press poll $100,000

Section 2.3.5. Academic Achievement. A maximum of one (1) of the following per Contract Year (payment based on highest goal achieved in this subsection):
   a. Single year APR of 980 or greater $100,000
   b. Single year APR of 960 or greater $50,000

Rick Barnes/University of Tennessee Employment Agreement, Amendment Number 1
Source: http://tennessee.edu/wp-content/uploads/2019/04/Rick-Barnes-basketball- am1.pdf

---

(Bonuses for head coach, women's volleyball)
   a. A maximum of one (1) of the following accomplishments (payment based on highest goal achieved in this subsection):
      i. Appearing in the NCAA Tournament   8% of Base Pay
      ii. Appearing in the NCAA Tournament Round of 16   12% of Base Pay
      iii. Winning the SEC Championship (regular season,
          as determined by the SEC, or tournament)   16% of Base Pay
      iv. Appearing in the NCAA Tournament Round of 8   16% of Base Pay
      v. Appearing in the NCAA Tournament Round of 4   20% of Base Pay
      vi. Winning the NCAA National Championship   24% Base Pay
   b. Coach is eligible to receive both incentive payments per Contract Year under this subsection:
      i. NCAA National Coach of the Year $5,000
      ii. SEC Coach of the Year $2,500

Eve Rackham/University of Tennessee Employment Agreement
Source: http://tennessee.edu/wp-content/uploads/2019/04/Eve-Rackham-volleyball.pdf

Coaches may also be awarded "retention bonuses" if they are employed through a certain date. These monetary incentives are built into coaching contracts to encourage coaches to remain at an institution over a period of time.

Retention Bonus: If Coach is employed as Head Men's Basketball Coach at University on September 1, 2020, University shall pay Coach $750,000 (Seven hundred fifty thousand dollars), such payment to be made on or before October 1, 2020.

Chris Beard/Texas Tech University Employment Agreement
Source: https://media.everythinglubbock.com/nxsglobal/everythinglubbock/document_dev/2019/04/29/Chris Beard - 2019_1556568389982_85046221_ver1.0.pdf

Termination

Coaches can be terminated "for cause." If a coach violates rules or breaches a provision of the contract, then the institution can fire the coach. When a termination for cause occurs, there no longer is any financial obligation on the part of the institution and payments will cease.

Coaches may also be terminated "without cause." This triggers what many refer to as the "buyout" provision. Liquidated damages allow both a coach and institution to negotiate a payment to be due if either party were to breach the contract. These payments should be negotiated in good faith to recognize the amount of damage the non-breaching party would incur in the event of termination.

The courts have enforced these liquidated damages clauses, but it must be a good faith estimate of the actual damages at the time the contract is signed, the amount cannot be merely a deterrence, and the amount cannot constitute a punishment. A reciprocal liquidated damages clause puts both parties in the same position for paying a buyout. (See *Vanderbilt University v. DiNardo*, 1999).

Termination Without Cause

A. Athletics shall have the right to terminate this Agreement without cause at any time upon written notice to Head Coach. In the event Athletics terminates this Agreement without cause, Athletics shall only be liable to Head Coach for the payment of liquidated damages as outlined in this section; no other sums or damages of any kind whatsoever shall be paid by Athletics to Head Coach.

David Beaty/University of Kansas Employment Agreement
Source: http://mediad.publicbroadcasting.net/p/kcur/files/david_beaty_2015_contract.pdf

(See also *Beaty v. Kansas Athletics, Inc.*, 2019, where Coach David Beaty sued the university for not paying him a $3 million buyout after he was fired without cause with three years remaining on his contract.)

Additional Terms

Duties

It is important carefully read the stated duties of a coach because a failure to perform such duties could constitute termination for cause. In fact, sometimes these duties are listed under the definition of "cause" in an employment agreement. The scope includes immoral, insubordinate, or incompetent behavior by the coach. This list is typically long and detailed. Some examples are

- serious violations of university, conference, or NCAA rules (Level I or II)
- refusal or inability to perform duties
- conviction of a serious criminal offense
- fraud, dishonesty, or moral turpitude
- misconduct (conduct that is detrimental to the best interests of the institution)
- failure of the coach to report promptly any compliance issue in which there is actual knowledge or reasonable cause to believe there is a violation
- failure to promote an atmosphere of compliance with respect to NCAA, conference, or university rules
- failure to report any Title IX violations
- providing false, misleading, or incomplete information for an investigation

Perquisites

The position of coach at many institutions comes with many "fringe benefits." The additional items that a coach receives because of being coach may include an automobile, phone, tickets, or country club membership. These are known as perquisites. It has been determined that these benefits align with the position of coach, and if there is a termination without cause, then the coach is entitled to the value of the perquisites for the remaining years of the contract, unless specifically excluded in the contract language (*Rodgers v. Georgia Tech Athletic Association*, 1983).

Perquisites have become a way to creatively attract and retain coaches through the provision of these fringe benefits.

> a. **Automobiles**
> Coach shall be provided with the use of two (2) late-model, quality automobiles for his official and personal use. In addition, the University shall reimburse Coach for all business related mileage consistent with the Athletics Department's standard operations.
>
> *John Calipari/University of Kentucky Employment Agreement*
> Source: https://www.uky.edu/legal/sites/www.uky.edu.legal/files/Coach_John_Calipari_Contract_0.pdf

> **SECTION 2.10. AIRCRAFT.** The University shall provide Coach with the use of noncommercial (private or charter) aircraft for Coach's personal, non-business travel, and/or that of his guests and/or family, for up to ten (10) round-trip flights within the continental United States per Contract Year. Coach acknowledges that the provision of aircraft for personal, non-business travel is a taxable fringe benefit subject to all applicable state and federal tax reporting and withholding requirements.
>
> *Rick Barnes/University of Tennessee Employment Agreement*
> Source: http://tennessee.edu/wp-content/uploads/2019/04/Rick-Barnes-basketball-am1.pdf

Reassignment

Instead of paying a buyout, some contracts will allow for a relocation of the coach to another position within the university. Generally, these provisions are disfavored for obvious reasons; however, the public policy reason is based on the idea that coaches should not be paid if they are not working. The reassignment clause allows a university to remove a coach from coaching duties and reassign them within the university system. If there is a reassignment clause, it should be narrowly tailored to include comparable positions or ones that the coach has the required skill to perform.

> b. KSA and the University retain the right to assign Coach to other positions with different duties during the term of this Agreement. If the University or KSA makes such a decision to reassign Coach and Coach refuses to accept such reassignment, then Coach's employment shall terminate pursuant to Section 4.01 of this Agreement. At any time during the term of this Agreement, Coach may be placed on administrative leave with pay at the discretion of KSA and/or University. If Coach is placed on administrative leave with pay at any time during his employment, he agrees that he will not accrue any additional vacation leave during the administrative leave period.
>
> *Bruce Weber/Kansas State University Employment Agreement*
> Source: http://mediad.publicbroadcasting.net/p/kcur/files/Bruce_Weber_Contract.pdf

Mitigation

Another option to try and alleviate the liquidated damages owed when a coach is terminated without cause is to require the coach to mitigate the damages by seeking employment. The duty to mitigate usually requires that the coach use reasonable efforts to secure a similar position. Some contracts are more specific as to the job that would be appropriate, such as another coaching position or broadcasting. The mitigation term may also require the coach to show the amount of pay, and that it must be pay reflective of the job market for that position. Therefore, a coach cannot take less pay for a job just because the university is paying the buyout.

a. Coach acknowledges and expressly agrees that he shall be required to mitigate any payments to him under Section 5.2.1;
b. Coach acknowledges and expressly agrees that he shall be required to make every reasonable and diligent effort as soon as practicable following his termination to seek and secure a Comparable Position. For purposes of this Agreement, the University shall determine whether a position constitutes a "Comparable Position" in its sole discretion, provided that a Comparable Position shall include other employment at the market rate for Division I collegiate basketball coaching positions or professional basketball coaching positions (a "Comparable Position"). Coach shall report monthly to the Director or the Director's designee on employment applications and progress in actively seeking other employment Coach shall notify Ohio State immediately if Coach has obtained other employment or has been engaged to provide services, either as an employee or an independent contractor. Coach's lack of diligence in seeking a Comparable Position or Coach's refusal of a reasonable offer of a Comparable Position voids Ohio State's responsibility to pay the Post-Termination Payments;

Chris Holtmann/The Ohio State University Employment Agreement
Source: http://media.cleveland.com/osu_impact/other/Chris%20Holtmann%20Employment%20Agreement%20-%20Fully%20Executed%20(00334073xB7A09).pdf

Future Trends in Coaching Contracts

Coaching contracts have become more sophisticated and complex. With higher salaries and expansive ranges of benefits (insurance policies, retention bonuses, deferred compensation, etc.) the expectations and responsibilities are increased as well. Some provisions that are increasingly likely to be found in the employment agreements are related to success rates, such as number of wins and participation in bowl games or the NCAA tournament. Also, there is more responsibility on the coach to behave in a manner that does not endanger student-athletes or promote a climate that is insensitive to harassment and discrimination.

Coaches are under intense scrutiny and the watchful eye of the public. They are paid exorbitant salaries in major college programs as well as the professional ranks. The significant pressure to win games and promote a positive image for the institution, donors, and sponsors are reflected in the compensation package in many college coaching contracts.

Case Notes: *Vanderbilt University v. DiNardo* (1999)

In December 1990, Gerry DiNardo was hired by Vanderbilt as football head coach for a term of 5 years. The employment contract stated the term was essential to the stability of the program, and it was agreed that if DiNardo resigned his position for another school before the term expired, he would pay Vanderbilt liquidated damages equal to his net salary for the time remaining on the contract. There was a reciprocal provision that required Vanderbilt to pay DiNardo if he was terminated by the University without cause. Prior to the expiration of the 5-year term, DiNardo accepted the head coaching job at Louisiana State University but refused to pay Vanderbilt the liquidated damages amount. Vanderbilt sued DiNardo and was granted summary judgment in its favor for the stated liquidated damage amount. The court left open a question of whether DiNardo owed Vanderbilt even more money, based on an addendum he signed for an additional 2-year contract extension, and remanded that for further proceedings.

Setting a Precedent

- *Vanderbilt University v. DiNardo*
- *Rodgers v. Georgia Tech Athletic Association*
- *Taylor v. Wake Forest University*
- *Levert v. University of Illinois*
- *Williamson v. Prime Sports Marketing*
- *Beaty v. Kansas Athletics, Inc.*

II. The Ethics

Case Scenarios

Case 1: *You are a college athletic director at X University (XU) in the Midwest. XU is about to commence its fall sports season, which includes football and other contact sports. At the same time, the Midwest is experiencing an outbreak of a contagious and life-threatening disease. The general counsel for XU recommends that, as a condition of their continued sport participation, all XU athletes must sign a waiver and release of liability in the event that they become ill or die from contracting the disease at any time during or after the fall season. Do you agree that this is the best ethical course forward for XU?*

Case 1 presents both legal and ethical dilemmas that college athletic programs faced during the COVID-19 pandemic. From a legal and risk management standpoint, the general counsel's advice is intended to reduce liability exposure for the university. Ethically, however, the use of a waiver and release in these circumstances is more problematic. First, for reasons discussed in Section I, such a waiver and release might be unenforceable and void as contrary to public policy. It is obviously a product of unfair and unequal bargaining power, as the student-athletes have little choice but to sign to ensure their ability to compete. Second, and equally important, is the ethical argument that the school is prioritizing financial gain from fall sports revenue over the health and safety of their student-athletes. The undue duress to give up legal rights to sue in these circumstances is morally and ethically wrong. Some would argue that even the decision to compete at all amid such serious health risks is ethically unsound, notwithstanding testing protocol and other protective measures.

During the COVID-19 pandemic, several schools were publicly criticized for proposing the use of waivers in these circumstances. At The Ohio State University (OSU), it was reported that student-athletes were asked to sign a waiver-like document acknowledging the risk of returning to play during the coronavirus pandemic (Baird, 2020). It was characterized in a more team-spirited and less legalistic way, however, as the apparent waiver was called the "Buckeye Acknowledgment and Pledge." While OSU did not expressly characterize this as a formal waiver and release, the language and mandatory signing of the "Pledge" reflects otherwise. The document contained the following language: "I understand that although the university is following the coronavirus guidelines issued by the CDC and other experts to reduce the spread of infection, I can never be completely shielded from all risk of illness caused by COVID-19 or other infections," and required the student-athlete's signature, as well as the signature of parents for those under the age of 18. This strongly suggests an effort to prevent legal liability through a binding legal document that was ethically if not legally improper. It was a mandatory requirement for participation that was at least partially intended to mitigate financial consequences to the university, despite being couched otherwise as a school-spirited "pledge." It is also reflective of an unfortunate trend of universities that attempt to shift liability to their student-athletes rather than taking all necessary steps and best practices to ensure their health and safety.

Case 2: *A premier college athlete at University Z (UZ) declares for the NBA draft and signs with an agent. A few weeks later, the athlete decides to sign with a more established and well-known agent and seeks to void his first contract, relying on the claim that the first agent was not registered in the state and his contract did not contain required language that the athlete would lose college eligibility upon signing with an agent. The first agent stands to lose millions of dollars in prospective earnings if the contract is voided, and reveals to the public that the athlete was not really an amateur to begin with, as he had been receiving improper benefits throughout his college career. Setting aside legal issues in this case, how would you evaluate the ethical decision-making of those involved in this scenario?*

Case 2 is modeled on the Zion Williamson case against Prime Sports Marketing, LLC, and agent Gina Ford. (See Case Notes above.) Williamson was an elite basketball player at Duke University, and during his freshman year he became a projected number one pick in the NBA draft. He declared for the NBA draft in April 2019, at which time he also signed a "marketing agent agreement" with sports agent Gina Ford and her company Prime Sports Marketing (PSM). Williamson later signed with another agency and sued in North Carolina to void his contract with PSM based on alleged violation of state unfair trade practices law, and specifically a violation of the North Carolina Uniform Athlete Agents Act (NCUAAA). The legal outcome in that case hinged, in part, on whether Williamson was truly an amateur athlete when he signed the contract. PSM asserted in a countersuit that he was not an amateur because he allegedly received improper benefits and inducements while at Duke. Ethically, it might appear that the athlete relied on a legal technicality to get out of his first deal and sign with a more high-profile and potentially more lucrative agency. While that legal technicality might be valid under the state athlete-agent law, it seems unlikely that the absence of the "loss of eligibility" warning in his contract made any difference to Williamson, as it was clear to all concerned that he would be turning professional at the end of his freshman year. The conduct of the agent, however, is also ethically questionable, as she promoted herself as a premier sports agent despite limited experience, failed to comply with the basic state law requirement of agent registration, and later sought to disclose potential NCAA rules violations committed by Williamson that, if true, she had previously concealed to her advantage. The roles of the competing agency and Duke also raise ethical questions in this scenario. Did the second agency intentionally interfere with PSM's business relationship for their own financial gain, and did Duke knowingly engage in improper benefits to Williamson, or turn a blind eye when it was occurring, to ensure Duke's competitive and financial success?

There is a long history of legal and ethical transgressions in the realm of sports agents. There are many examples of unscrupulous agents who take advantage of unsuspecting young athletes for their own personal and financial gain. At the same time, we have seen examples of third parties, including coaches and universities, that were complicit in flouting amateur rules regarding improper benefits, and are not deserving of the protections under state athlete-agent laws. Finally, some athletes simply choose whatever means they can to avoid paying earned fees and commissions to their agents, in violation of their contractual agreement and ethical responsibilities.

Throughout its history, the NCAA has steadfastly maintained its founding principle of amateurism in intercollegiate athletics. This is rooted in the notion that athletics has as its primary core an educational mission for student-athletes. This principle has been challenged of late from both legal and ethical standpoints. Legally, it is argued that the NCAA restrictions on student-athlete outside employment and endorsement income related to their athletic talents are an illegal restraint of trade, in violation of federal antitrust laws. Ethically, it is argued that student-athletes are being exploited when their schools and universities are profiting from their athletic team success and the popularity of individual star athletes, who themselves are precluded from accepting money, beyond their scholarship grants, for their own name, image, and likeness. The ethical failures are especially pronounced when the student-athletes do not actually receive the education they were promised, when schools circumvent academic standards to ensure athletic eligibility, as exemplified in a major scandal at UNC–Chapel Hill, described in Case 3 below. Scandals like this, as well as popular opinion trends favoring fair treatment for athletes, have led to recently proposed state and federal legislation in this area, and the easing of NCAA amateurism rules.

Case 3: *For nearly 20 years, football and basketball players at University of North Carolina at Chapel Hill (UNC) were steered by academic advisors into taking so-called "paper classes." These classes, designated as independent study courses within an academic unit at UNC, involved no interaction with any faculty, and no required class attendance or coursework other than a single paper. The papers were favorably "graded," regardless of quality or content, by a secretary within the department, who helped initiate the system to assist UNC athletes. The courses were specifically set up to benefit student-athletes with poor academic performance, by handing out consistently high grades to ensure that they maintained their academic eligibility for continued sport participation. Eventually, the courses were made available to non-athletes and became popular among fraternities across campus. The academic fraud was unraveled by a whistleblower named Mary Willingham, who was a learning specialist at UNC. She went public with the ongoing scheme and made her opinions known that the student-athletes involved were not being well-served or properly educated by the university. According to the university-commissioned Wainstein investigation, this was a "shadow curriculum" of fake classes into which athletes were steered that went on for nearly two decades. In 2015, the NCAA undertook an investigation but concluded, in 2017, that there were no specific NCAA rules violations and no penalties would be imposed on UNC.*

Case 3 is a real-life scandal that occurred at a prestigious university with a prominent athletics program and legacy. It was revealed that for decades the internal academic systems allowed underprepared basketball and football players to take fake courses and, in turn, earn devalued degrees. According to an athletics department whistleblower and a follow-up independent investigation, UNC athletes, particularly those in "revenue" sports, were referred to these classes by academic counselors in UNC's Academic Support Program for Student-Athletes, who were under pressure to maintain student-athlete eligibility. They saw these fake classes with artificially high grades as the key to "helping" academically challenged athletes remain eligible (Wainstein et al., 2014). It was subsequently evident that certain coaches, faculty, administrators, and university officials were knowingly involved or simply looked the other way while this fraud was perpetrated, prioritizing athletic team success and millions of dollars in sports revenues.

From a contractual standpoint, it seems apparent that the student-athletes did not receive what they were promised; that is, an education at a top university. Arguably, every university engaging in this type of academic fraud commits a breach of terms of scholarship agreements, which promise the opportunity to receive a valuable college education (Smith and Willingham, 2015). Yet there were no successful lawsuits against UNC on this legal theory. And, even more remarkably, the NCAA in 2017 determined that it would not punish the university or its athletics program because the "paper classes" were not exclusively available to athletes. Because other students at UNC had access to the fraudulent classes as well, the NCAA concluded that there was no specific violation of NCAA academic rules. Further, while NCAA Bylaw 10.1 prohibits unethical conduct by student-athletes and institutional staff members, there were no adverse findings or penalties imposed under that rule. This was a significant victory for the UNC, as they faced severe financial and reputational consequences, including the loss of past championships in men's basketball, which has been its signature and possibly most lucrative sport, and a source of great pride and success among alums, donors, and sponsors. The NCAA was widely criticized for its ruling in this case. It revealed the hypocrisy of the NCAA's continued insistence upon amateurism to promote the central tenet of education in intercollegiate athletics. Instead, the NCAA gave a pass that allowed a major program to continue its revenue model at the obvious expense of the education of their student-athletes.

Ethically, the magnitude of this scandal and the lack of punishment by the national governing body demonstrate a violation of trust in our system of higher education. At all levels of the university, the ethical decision-making favored big-time athletic success and the related publicity and revenues. The widespread numbers of individuals who were complicit in facilitating the fraud included academic advisers, coaches, faculty, staff, administrators, and officials, yet UNC received no meaningful penalties from its athletic conference or the NCAA. One ethical concept that applies to this scandal is incrementalism, which is the "slippery slope" that may cause people to commit increasingly serious unethical behavior (*Ethics Unwrapped*. https://ethicsunwrapped.texas.edu). Those who engage in wrongdoing, such as the athletic advisers who initially simply recommended one class to a particular student-athlete, may not have started with the idea and intent to commit massive academic fraud over a period of decades. That individual more likely began by rationalizing one situation and then sliding into further participation over time and degree, perhaps not fully realizing the major ethical lapse. Another ethical concept that applies to this scandal is called conformity bias. That is the tendency of people to behave like others around them, rather than using their own best judgment. Some people may see others succeeding by cheating, and it makes them more likely to cheat themselves. They act unethically because "everyone else is doing it," rather than using their own independent judgment. This applies to some student-athletes and others who knowingly took the classes, voluntarily, with the specific intent to get good grades and "game" the system. In those instances, it might be argued that the student-athletes were not necessarily "cheated" by their university, as they were willing participants in the "cheating" themselves. They knew the paper classes were wrong but justified taking them because their peers were doing the exact same thing.

Closing Arguments

It is essential that sport managers understand the fundamental principles of contract law and the many types of contracts prevalent in the sport industry. Many legal disputes and lawsuits arise when parties fail to act in good faith or perform their duties or obligations as promised. The law provides a cause of action for remedies and damages when parties commit a breach of contract. Ethics also play a role in negotiating and enforcing contracts. Unfortunately, as with all businesses, the sport industry has experienced its share of bad actors, who utilize questionable practices, such as inequitable and unfair waivers and releases or one-sided athlete representation contracts. Finally, in intercollegiate athletics, we are in the midst of significant legislative reforms at the state and federal levels as a result of the perceived hypocrisy of the NCAA and the exploitation of scholarship athletes under the guise of amateurism.

Study Questions

1. What are the required elements of contract formation and the legal remedies and available damages for breach of contract?
2. Describe the circumstances that lead to a university's obligation to pay a departing coach a "buyout."
3. Why might a participation waiver and release not be enforceable in court? What factors are key in drafting an effective waiver and release?
4. Discuss the ethical decision-making issues faced by an institution scheduled to compete in football in the Big Ten Conference during the COVID-19 pandemic.
5. Do you think that the student-athletes at UNC who took "paper classes" were cheating or cheated? Discuss the ethical failures at all levels of the university in that scandal.

Title IX and Sex Discrimination in Sport

CHAPTER 4

Opening Statement

Historically, sport opportunities for girls and women were very limited. There are many sociocultural, political, and legal explanations for this. In some cases, the lack of opportunities and resources for girls in sport was rooted in discriminatory bias and stereotypes, for example, the widespread belief that girls and women were too fragile or too weak to play, or the unsupported notion that girls and women lack interest in sports and athletic competition. For many years, schools and universities formed athletic programs based upon those biases and stereotypes. In doing so, they were also mindful of financial constraints, and allocated nearly all athletic resources and sport opportunities only to boys and men. There were no state or federal laws specifically aimed to remedy such inequities and, as a result, the systematic exclusion and disparate treatment of girls and women in sport typically went unchallenged in the courts.

After 1972, sport opportunities and resources for girls and women significantly began to change in the United States due the enactment of a landmark civil rights law known as Title IX. These changes were first reflected in the dramatic increase in participation numbers for girls and women in high school and college athletics. Over time, girls and women also began receiving equitable treatment and benefits in those athletic programs, in comparison to their male counterparts. Today, five decades after its enactment, Title IX is also considered responsible for major social and cultural changes in sport, including the widespread acceptance of women as athletes and the recognition of women as potential leaders in the sport industry.

Section I of this chapter examines the legal aspects of Title IX in athletics, including its legislative history and implementing regulations. It addresses key legal developments as well as common misconceptions about the legal requirements and potential liability of schools and universities with respect to athletic compliance. In addition, this section focuses on how and why Title IX applies to sexual harassment and sexual assault in a school sports context,

LEARNING OBJECTIVES

After reading this chapter, students will:

1. Understand the history of Title IX and its application to sex discrimination in sport
2. Know the requirements for athletic compliance under Title IX and how the law is enforced
3. Understand how Title IX applies to sexual harassment and sexual assault in athletic programs at schools and universities
4. Recognize the potential legal liability of schools and universities in Title IX lawsuits
5. Consider the ethical implications of sex-testing in sport
6. Understand the legal and ethical issues surrounding transgender athletes
7. Recognize the ethical failures in institutional cover-ups of sexual assault and sexual abuse

for example, when alleged perpetrators or victims of sexual misconduct are student-athletes, coaches, or other team personnel. Other federal laws that govern sex discrimination in employment, including sex-based wage disparities in sport organizations and sexual harassment in the workplace, are addressed later, in Chapter 5, Employment Law and Diversity in Sport Organizations.

Section II of this chapter addresses many ethical questions related to sex discrimination in sport. For example, why are schools reluctant or slow to comply with Title IX in athletics? Is it ethical for an athletic director to circumvent Title IX regulations because of budgetary constraints, or because they believe the law will not be vigorously enforced? Similarly, there are ethical issues related to treatment of transgender athletes. What are the appropriate team assignments for transgender athletes in an athletic program which offers only men's and women's teams or events? Also, in that context, is it reasonable or ethical for schools and sport organizations to implement "sex-testing" in women's sports to ensure competitive fairness among all participants? Finally, there have been major scandals involving cover-ups of sexual assault in college athletic programs and sexual abuse in youth sports. Aside from the legal implications of those cases, how do we analyze or explain the ethical failures of those in positions of authority who turned a blind eye to sexual misconduct at the expense of the victims?

I. The Law

Title IX

Title IX is a federal civil rights law that was passed by Congress as part of the Education Amendments of 1972 (20 U.S.C. §§ 1681–1688). Title IX states, **"No person in the United States shall, on the basis of sex, be excluded from participation in, be denied the benefits of, or be subjected to discrimination under any education program or activity receiving Federal financial assistance."** Notably, the language of the statute does not expressly mention athletics, but rather addresses sex discrimination throughout educational institutions. However, athletic programs in schools at all levels are considered "education programs or activities," and thus are covered under Title IX.

For many years, it was unclear how Title IX would specifically apply to school athletic programs and how it would be enforced. In 1975, the federal regulations governing Title IX athletic compliance were formally issued and high schools and colleges were given three years within which to comply (34 C.F.R. Part 106). In 1979, the U.S. Department of Health, Education, and Welfare (HEW) issued its final policy interpretation, entitled "Title IX and Intercollegiate Athletics." In 1980, the U.S. Department of Education (DOE) was established with oversight responsibility for Title IX enforcement through its federal agency known as the Office for Civil Rights (OCR). The subsections below highlight the legislative history of Title IX, key legal and policy developments associated with its applicability to athletics, and its application to sexual misconduct in schools.

Legislative History

The legislative history of Title IX is broad and complex. First, it is important to understand the legal, social, and political climate at the time Title IX was debated and passed into law. Prior to 1972, there was widespread discrimination against women in many areas of education. For example, there were quotas limiting the admission of women in higher education in fields such as law, medicine, engineering, and science, which were traditionally viewed as male professions. Such quotas served to favor male applicants, regardless of their qualifications. Similarly, qualified women were often not hired, promoted, or even considered for faculty or administrative positions at many schools and universities, because those positions had always been reserved for men. Title IX was enacted to prohibit such discriminatory practices and all other forms of sex-based discrimination in educational programs and activities at institutions that received federal funds. It was modeled after another federal civil rights law—Title VI—which prohibits discrimination based on race, color, and national origin in programs and activities receiving federal financial assistance (42 U.S.C. § 2000d, *et. seq.*, 1964). In a similar fashion, Title IX was passed as a "non-discrimination" statute that extends to sex. Importantly, although history reflects that women and girls were often excluded or unfairly treated in education when Title IX was enacted, the law on its face protects both men and women from discrimination through the express language "based on sex."

Early Cases and Policy Developments

In an early legal challenge to Title IX itself, a small, private college in California claimed that Title IX applied only if the specific educational program at issue directly received federal funds. The U.S. Supreme Court ruled in favor of the college, thus adopting a very narrow "programmatic" approach to Title IX's applicability and enforcement (*Grove City College v. Bell,* 1984). That case led to widespread noncompliance with Title IX in athletics, as schools asserted that their athletic departments did not directly receive federal funds and were therefore exempt. However, the limited scope of the Grove City interpretation was soon overturned and expressly rejected by Congress through the enactment of a new law, over President Reagan's veto, named the Civil Rights Restoration Act of 1987 (Pub. L. 100-259). That law clarified and established an "institutional" approach for Title IX; that is, that all schools, public and private, are bound if the institution itself receives federal funds, regardless of where those funds are directed. In fact, today, most public and private institutions receive some form of federal funding, for example, via student loans, academic research, scientific grants, or other types of financial assistance, and are therefore bound by Title IX in all their educational programs and activities. There are a very small number of schools that refuse to accept any federal funds at all. Under those circumstances, the institution would be exempt from Title IX.

Title IX's application to athletics was controversial and the subject of many legal challenges. On the one hand, it was obvious that school athletic programs (not unlike math, science, band, drama, or other extracurriculars) were educational programs and activities within the meaning of Title IX. Yet, from the outset, there was considerable opposition to the passage and enforcement of Title IX, particularly because of its potential application to intercollegiate athletics. Various schools, universities, athletic directors, and football coaches believed that equal opportunities and fair treatment for women in athletics would necessarily diminish opportunities for men and lead to the downfall or elimination of major college football. Athletic directors feared that financial constraints would make it impossible to maintain competitive men's programs in all sports if their athletic budgets were reallocated to develop and support women's teams. Some argued that creating new opportunities for women was not feasible due to a lack of facilities and staffing, and that the law was simply too burdensome. There was well-organized opposition to Title IX based on these arguments, including major political and legal efforts to narrow the interpretation of the law and its implementing regulations.

In 1974, college athletic directors and football coaches lobbied Congress and President Gerald Ford to expressly exclude athletics from Title IX via the so-called "Tower Amendment," which ultimately failed to pass. There were other lobbying efforts by Title IX opponents to specifically exempt football or revenue sports from Title IX, but those efforts were also unsuccessful. One of the first major organizations to take legal action was the National Collegiate Athletic Association (NCAA), which at the time was the national governing body for men's intercollegiate sports. In 1976, the NCAA filed a federal lawsuit challenging the legality of Title IX's application to intercollegiate athletics, but its claims seeking to invalidate the federal regulations were rejected and the case was eventually dismissed (*National Collegiate Athletic Association v. Joseph Califano*, 1978). At the time, women's athletics were governed by the Association for Intercollegiate Athletics for Women (AIAW). After losing its legal challenge to Title IX, the NCAA authorized a committee directed to examine and make recommendations regarding potential governance of women's athletics for its member institutions. The AIAW then sued the NCAA, contending that its expansion into women's athletics was an unlawful use of its monopoly power in violation of federal antitrust laws. By 1982, all divisions of the NCAA offered national championship events for women's teams and the AIAW discontinued its operations. The AIAW's lawsuit was ultimately decided in favor of the NCAA, with the court finding no antitrust violation (*AIAW v. NCAA*, 1984).

Since 1980, the OCR has issued various policy interpretations and policy clarifications of Title IX, in the form of "Dear Colleague Letters." These are not binding law, but they provide advisory guidance to schools and universities on Title IX compliance requirements, including athletics. (See Figure 4.4.) The OCR most recently updated its comprehensive policy guidance for athletics in 2010 (OCR Dear Colleague Letter, 2010). As discussed further below, the OCR later issued policy guidance in areas of sexual assault and transgender status that would also impact the administration of school athletic programs.

Anyone may file a Title IX complaint with the OCR against a school or institution and, if desired, may do so anonymously. The OCR then evaluates the facts and allegations and determines whether a full program investigation is warranted. The ultimate penalty by the DOE for noncompliance with Title IX is the withdrawal of federal funds from the noncompliant institution. Although a substantial majority of schools and colleges are still not in compliance with Title IX as applied to athletics, the withdrawal of federal funds has never been imposed by the DOE. Instead, when an institution is investigated and determined to be out of compliance with Title IX's athletic regulations, the OCR typically enters into a voluntary resolution agreement outlining the specific measures required to remedy the identified problems. The OCR is then responsible for monitoring that the institution implements those measures. Critics have noted that in many past cases involving Title IX noncompliance in athletics, the OCR has been lax in its ongoing monitoring and enforcement responsibilities, due in part to the lack of continuity in OCR policy guidance and the changing enforcement priorities under new political administrations (Thomas, 2011).

In addition to the administrative remedy available through OCR complaints, the U.S. Supreme Court ruled that an individual has a private cause of action under Title IX (*Cannon v. University of Chicago*, 1979). This means that an individual may file a lawsuit in federal court against their school if they are a victim of discrimination under Title IX. Thirteen years after *Cannon*, in another landmark case, the U.S. Supreme Court unanimously ruled that money damages and attorney fees are recoverable for plaintiffs who prove intentional Title IX violations in federal court actions (*Franklin v. Gwinnett County Public Schools*, 1992). This opened the door to many more lawsuits on behalf of plaintiffs, usually women, who were denied sport participation opportunities. After *Franklin*, those women could seek monetary compensation from their educational institutions for violations of Title IX. Another landmark case was decided in 2005, when the U.S. Supreme Court ruled that it is illegal for schools to retaliate against coaches or others who complain of Title IX violations (*Jackson v. Birmingham Board of Education*, 2005). After that decision, many successful lawsuits were brought by coaches and administrators against their schools based on allegations that they were fired because of their prior Title IX complaints or advocacy.

Amid these major cases, there were continuing political efforts to review, revise, or potentially repeal Title IX. Many believed that Title IX was still flawed in its application to athletics and was too burdensome on schools. Others argued that the law was no longer necessary and had fully served its purpose by increasing athletic opportunities for women. In 2002, President George W. Bush created a Commission on Opportunity in Athletics and convened congressional hearings to debate the proper scope of Title IX regulations and the future of the law. This resulted in modest changes through further policy guidance but no material changes to the import of the law. Another legal effort challenging the scope of Title IX was thereafter initiated by the National Wrestling Coaches Association (NWCA), which sued the DOE seeking to invalidate the athletic compliance regulations. The NWCA asserted, in part, that Title IX requirements were unlawfully applied, causing harm to men's wrestling programs, which had been eliminated at various schools. The NWCA case was unsuccessful and dismissed by the U.S. District Court, and the U.S. Supreme Court later declined to hear an appeal (*National Wrestling Coaches Association v. U.S. Department of Education*, 2003). As is further discussed below, the legal argument that Title IX mandates the elimination of men's sports has been consistently rejected by the federal courts. In such cases, contrary to arguments raised by the NWCA and other like-minded groups, courts have found that athletic departments make independent decisions about which teams they offer or eliminate based on a variety of factors, including finances, which do not include sex. In fact, under Title IX policy guidance, the cutting of men's teams is a disfavored practice to achieve equity and fairness.

More recently, in 2016, the OCR provided additional guidance to schools by interpreting "sex" under Title IX to also include transgender status or gender identity (OCR Dear Colleague Letter, 2016). OCR policy guidance, however, is not binding law, and that 2016 guidance was rescinded by the Trump administration the very next year. At the time of writing, the full scope of the definition of "sex" under Title IX remains a matter for court interpretation. In fact, antidiscrimination protection for transgender athletes has been controversial and the subject of many legal challenges. As discussed later in Chapter 5, the U.S. Supreme Court recently interpreted "sex" to include transgender persons in a case arising under a different law—Title VII of the Civil Rights Act of 1964—which prohibits sex discrimination in employment (42 U.S.C. § 2000d, *et. seq.*). The U.S. Supreme Court has not yet addressed whether the Title VII definition of "sex" should be extended to Title IX. This will be a critical legal question in future Title IX cases involving transgender athletes.

Athletic Compliance Regulations

There are three components of Title IX as it applies to athletics programs: (a) effective accommodation of student interests and abilities ("Participation"), (b) athletic financial assistance ("Scholarships"), and (c) other program components ("Treatment"). To achieve athletic compliance, institutions must meet requirements in all three areas as follows.

Participation

Participation deals with overall sport and athletic participation offerings available for men and women. A school is deemed to be in participation compliance if it satisfies any *one* of the following three standards, in what is known as the "three-prong test":

1. Males and females participate in athletics in numbers "substantially proportionate" to their respective undergraduate enrollments; *or*
2. The institution shows a "history and continuing practice of program expansion" which is demonstrably responsive to the developing interests and abilities of members of the underrepresented sex; *or*
3. The "interests and abilities" of the underrepresented sex are "fully and effectively accommodated" by the existing programs.

The three-prong test was issued by HEW in its 1979 policy interpretation setting forth Title IX enforcement requirements. This test was subsequently applied by federal courts in many Title IX cases that alleged a denial of athletic participation opportunities based on sex. Much of the case law interpreting Title IX arose in this area of participation, pursuant to claims brought by girls or women who were underrepresented or denied sport opportunities in their schools. In 1996, the three-prong test was reaffirmed as the correct legal standard of review for such claims by the United States Court of Appeals for the 1st Circuit (*Cohen v. Brown University*, 1996). (See also Case Notes.)

Under prong one, the meaning of "substantially proportionate" has long been the subject of debate and different interpretations. To illustrate how the first prong is applied at a particular institution, one must first examine the ratio of undergraduate enrollment by sex. If, for example, a school's undergraduate enrollment is 55% male and 45% female, then under the first prong you would expect approximately 55% of its athletes are male, and approximately 45% of its athletes are female. To date, the OCR has not determined an exact percentage variance in that ratio that would constitute noncompliance under prong one. In early Title IX athletic compliance investigations, the OCR permitted variances as high as 5%. In a 1996 policy interpretation, however, it was suggested that no more that 2% is allowable, taking into consideration that exact proportionality is desired but that undergraduate enrollment numbers are subject to fluctuation from year to year, which may impact the ratio for reasons that are nondiscriminatory.

Under prong two, a school must demonstrate a history and continuing practice of program expansion. This includes adding teams, resources, and/or scholarships for the underrepresented sex. In the first few decades after Title IX was passed, some schools successfully relied upon this prong to demonstrate participation compliance, in circumstances where their participation numbers were far outside the proportionality ratio (See, e.g., *Boucher v. Syracuse University*, 1999). However, it is increasingly unlikely that this defense will succeed today, 50 years after Title IX was passed, if schools claim a continuing practice of expansion yet still cannot demonstrate equitable progress on participation opportunities.

Under prong three, a school must demonstrate that it has fully and effectively accommodated the interests and abilities of the underrepresented sex. Key factors that the OCR considers under this standard include reliable surveys of athletic interest, reviews of club and intramural sport participation levels, tracking high school and amateur sport offerings in local communities, and interviews and meetings with students, prospective students, and coaches regarding athletic interest. Notably, in the *Cohen* case mentioned above, Brown University had demoted two women's teams from university-funded to donor-funded status. In the lawsuit filed by members of the women's teams, Brown was unable to satisfy any of the three prongs in the applicable test but offered a "relative interest" survey in support of its argument that women at Brown were less interested in sports than men. The Court rejected the survey and this defense, noting that Brown could not excuse its failure to accommodate the interest and ability of the women athletes through outdated stereotypes about women, and stated more broadly that "interest and ability rarely develop in a vacuum; they evolve as a function of opportunity and experience" (*Cohen,* at 179).

Scholarships

This Title IX requirement pertains to athletic scholarships in intercollegiate programs. Scholarship dollars must be allocated in proportion to the number of female and male students participating in intercollegiate athletics. Scholarship funding for men's and women's programs does not have to be equal, but the OCR guidance allows no more than a 1% variance in determining proportionality under this requirement, unless justified by nondiscriminatory factors, to be determined on a case-by-case basis (OCR Dear Colleague Letter to Bowling Green State University, July 23, 1998). A possible nondiscriminatory factor to justify a greater variance might occur, for example, if a men's program at a public institution happened to have more out-of-state athletes overall in a particular year. In those circumstances, there would be higher tuition expenses for the male scholarship athletes due to the school's tuition residency requirements, which apply equally to all students. In that example, assuming the school does not restrict recruitment of out-of-state female athletes, the variance between male and female scholarship dollars might exceed 1% and would be permissible because it is not "based on sex."

Treatment

This Title IX requirement addresses treatment in other athletic benefits and opportunities. It covers 11 program areas, referred to by the OCR as the "laundry list," to determine equivalence of overall treatment. The regulations do not mandate that each men's and women's program receive identical treatment. Rather, the OCR has determined that the men's and women's programs, in their entirety, should receive equivalent treatment—that is, the same level and quality of service, facilities, and supplies—in the following areas: (a) equipment and supplies; (b) scheduling of games and practice times; (c) travel and daily allowance; (d) opportunity to receive coaching; (e) academic tutoring; (f) locker rooms, practice, and competitive facilities; (g) provision of medical training facilities and services; (h) provision of housing and dining facilities and services; (i) publicity; (j) recruitment of student-athletes; and (k) support services. The standard is one of "quality" as opposed to dollar amounts spent.

Under this requirement, sport-to-sport comparisons are useful for analysis and identifying differences in benefits, but compliance determinations are dependent upon a comparison of the total women's program to the total men's program. Minor disparities do not necessarily constitute a Title IX violation;

however, they are reviewed collectively to determine whether they create a pattern and practice of discriminatory treatment that would violate Title IX.

Case Notes: *Cohen v. Brown University*

In 1991, Brown University faced budget constraints in their athletic program. They decided to demote four sports from "university-funded" (varsity) status to "donor-funded" (club) status. Brown contended that their decision was fair and even-handed from a gender equity perspective, because they demoted two women's sports (volleyball and gymnastics), and two men's sports (golf and water polo). Brown's decision slightly reduced the percentage of female student-athlete opportunities from 36.7% to 36.6% percent. When compared to the full-time undergraduate student enrollment ratio by sex (47.6% women, 52.4 % men), this resulted in an 11% participation disparity. In response, members of the women's volleyball and gymnastics teams filed a class-action Title IX lawsuit against Brown, claiming that the program eliminations placed the university even further out of participation compliance.

After an initial injunction hearing, the federal district court ordered Brown to reinstate the two women's teams to varsity status pending the outcome of the case. On appeal, the court recognized that it must interpret the requirements of Title IX in an athletics context on a comprehensive basis for the first time. In its ruling, the court quickly concluded that Brown could not satisfy prongs one or two of the three-prong test, noting that an 11% differential was too great of a disparity under prong one; and the absence of any program expansion in the last 12 years was insufficient under the second prong. The court then examined the third prong, which requires a showing by the plaintiffs that the interests and abilities of the underrepresented have not been fully and effectively accommodated by the sport offerings within the present athletics program.

Brown argued that colleges should only be required to accommodate the students' athletics interests in direct proportion to their comparative level of interest. Brown maintained that compliance is achieved if athletics opportunities were afforded to women in accordance with the ratio of interested and able women to interested and able men. Brown disregarded the relative percentage of women among the full-time undergraduate population and instead used as the comparator the percentage of interested and able women. The court rejected this "relative interests" approach. Instead, it found that effective accommodation requires an accurate assessment of whether there is unmet need in the underrepresented gender. Because Brown was cutting varsity opportunities that existed for women, it was not effectively accommodating "interests and abilities" under prong three. After years of litigation, the court ordered that Brown reinstate the women's teams with funding, coaching, and other benefits comparable to their men's varsity teams.

Overall Impact and Misconceptions

The impact of Title IX on women in sport is undeniable. Yet, there are still many misconceptions surrounding the specific application of Title IX to athletic programs. To examine the overall impact, as well as the common myths and inaccuracies about its application to sport, it is important to understand the basic premise. As noted above, Title IX is a nondiscrimination civil rights law; it is not a mandate to impose "affirmative action" or statistical quotas. It provides civil rights protection to ensure that men and women are treated in a like manner with regard to all educational programs and activities, including athletics. Quite simply, as to athletics, if a school chooses to offer and administer an athletic program, Title IX requires that it do so fairly between men and women.

Relevant historical data from governing bodies for high school and intercollegiate athletics reflect the dramatic impact of Title IX on increasing participation opportunities for female athletes. (See Figures 4.1 and 4.2, "Touch Points in History.") Prior to 1972, approximately 1 in 27 high school girls played sports; that number today is closer to 1 in 2. The National Federation of High Schools (NFHS) Athletics Participation Survey shows 294,015 girls participated in high school athletics in 1971–72; as of 2018–19, that number was roughly 3.4 million (www.nfhs.org/sports-resource-content/high-school-participation-survey-archive/). Those girls who did compete in high school athletics prior to Title IX also experienced a severe lack of resources and inequitable funding. Similarly, at the intercollegiate level, pre-Title IX participation opportunities for women were less than 30,000,

Touch Points in History
High School Athletics Participation Survey Totals 1971-72-2018-19

FIGURE 4.1 *Historical Participation Data (Men/Women): High School Athletics*
Source: National Federation of State High School Associations 2018–19 Athletics Participation Summary.

Touch Points in History
College Sports Participation 1971-72-2017-18

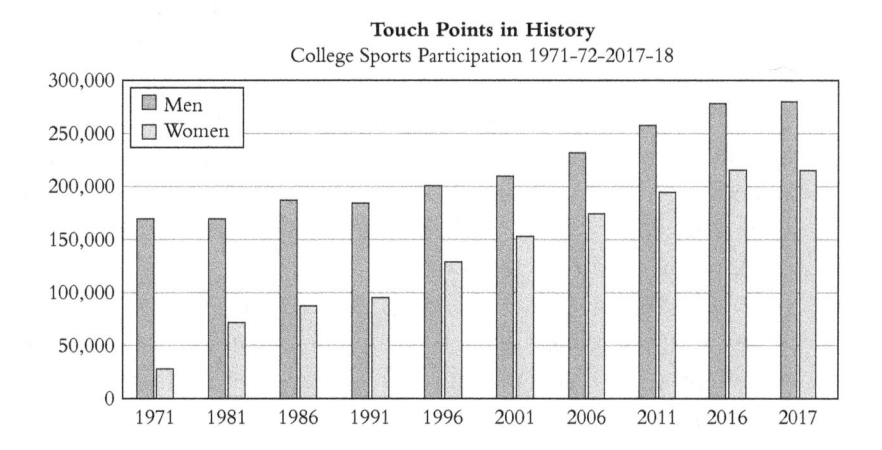

FIGURE 4.2 *Historical Participation Data (Men/Women): Intercollegiate Athletics*
Source: NCAA Sponsorship & Participation Rates Report 1981–82–2017–18.

with a total of 50 athletic scholarships available, and limited resources for those who were able to participate. Recent data from the NCAA reflects women's participation numbers at 221,042 across Divisions I, II, and III, as of 2018–19, with many schools offering scholarship opportunities proportionate to overall participation (NCAA Sports Spornsorship and Participation Rates Report, Rev. January 6, 2022).

These dramatic changes did not occur because girls and women suddenly developed a new interest in sports, or because schools and their athletic directors decided it was time to treat girls and women fairly. Rather, Title IX was a necessary legal impetus to effectively remedy sex-based discrimination in school athletic programs. Title IX also led to major sociocultural changes in the perception of women as athletes and coaches, and as sport managers and administrators. Overall, the law helped break barriers for women in sport and the sport industry at large. From a broader sociological perspective, Title IX led to a new understanding and rejection of deep-seated and unfounded stereotypes about girls and women, in general, that had been used to justify their marginalization and exclusion from male-dominated and male-identified fields such as sports.

So, while its impact is clear, nearly 50 years after its enactment, much of Title IX and its application to athletics remains fundamentally misunderstood. First among the many myths and misconceptions is the idea that Title IX imposes quotas for women. In fact, as all federal courts that have examined this issue have concluded, Title IX does not require quotas; it simply requires that schools allocate participation opportunities in a nondiscriminatory fashion. Schools may achieve participation compliance by satisfying any one of the requirements in the three-prong test, without any mandated quota (National Women's Law Center, 2017).

Another misconception is that Title IX requires the elimination of men's sports. In fact, the elimination of any sport is a disfavored practice under Title IX; the intent and language of the regulations is to increase opportunities for the underrepresented sex. It is true that some schools, for financial reasons, have chosen to eliminate certain men's sports, such as gymnastics or wresting, yet that choice is often made in lieu of other options, such as reducing exorbitant expenses and salaries in the "arms race" in another men's sport, such as football or basketball. Notably, opportunities for boys and men have continued to increase in other sports (e.g., soccer and lacrosse), based on the increasing popularity of those sports across the country. Overall participation data from 1972 to date confirms that the number of opportunities for boys and men in school athletics programs has not diminished since the enactment of Title IX. Instead, while the participation gap has significantly narrowed between male and female athletes in high school and college, with more opportunities for girls and women, the majority of all sport opportunities are still allocated to boys in high school sports and to men in college sports, regardless of the underlying student enrollment ratio by sex.

There is also the common myth that Title IX mandates parallel sport offerings and/or identical budgets and expenditures. This is untrue, as schools may choose to offer whatever teams they wish and there is a built-in recognition under the law that some sports are more expensive than others. Under Title IX participation and treatment requirements, compliance is assessed through a total program comparison. In an OCR investigation of a complaint, the entire men's and women's programs are compared, not just one men's team to the women's team in the same sport. This broad comparative approach emphasizes that Title IX does not require the creation of mirror image programs. Males and females may participate in different sports according to their respective interests and abilities.

Finally, under Title IX participation compliance, there are no sport exclusions or exceptions, and therefore football is included in the participation count. Individual participation opportunities in all men's sports and all women's sports are counted to determine whether a school meets the Title IX participation standard; the number of men's and women's teams is not relevant to that analysis. And although it is a fact that most college football programs lose money, a school may not assert potential revenue production as a justification to provide more opportunities or better treatment for male athletes. Under Title IX, a civil rights law, there is no economic justification that would allow sex-based discrimination in any educational programs, including athletics.

Key Legal Developments and OCR Guidance

Figures 4.3 and 4.4 summarize, by substance and date, key legal developments over several decades following the enactment of Title IX (Figure 4.3), as well as the guidance provided by the OCR to schools through Dear Colleague Letters as to how the regulations should be implemented (Figure 4.4). The cases listed in Figure 4.3 were all decided by the U.S. Supreme Court and contain important rulings on the scope and application of Title IX. The federal statutes listed in Figure 4.3 are also important for understanding the changes and progress after Title IX's enactment. The first federal statute, the Civil Rights Restoration Act, is explained above in the Legislative History section. Another important federal law, the Equity in Athletics Disclosure Act (EADA), was passed by Congress to mandate that colleges and universities annually report to the DOE on their athletics programs regarding participation by sex, staffing, revenues, and expenses (Pub. L. No. 105-244). That information is publicly available in a database on the EADA website (http://www.ope.ed.gov/athletics/#/) and is an important oversight tool for the OCR in its enforcement function.

Figure 4.4 reflects Title IX guidance from the OCR under the Obama administration during the period from 2010 to 2016 and denotes (in red) the withdrawal or rescission of such guidance under the Trump administration in 2017. This has led to much uncertainty in the current scope and application of Title IX, including whether sex discrimination under Title IX includes discrimination based on transgender status or gender identity. As discussed above, the U.S. Supreme Court has not yet ruled on this issue. Notably, many states have adopted laws to preclude or limit transgender participation in women's sports based on the assertion that such participation contravenes the legislative intent of Title IX. The ethical aspects of such laws are addressed further in Section II, Case 2 herein.

1979	HEW Policy Interpretation: "Three-Prong Test"
1979	*Cannon v. University of Chicago* (individual right to sue)
1980	Dept. of Education/Office for Civil Rights
1984	*Grove City College v. Bell* (program/institution)
1988	Civil Rights Restoration Act
1992	*Franklin v. Gwinnett County Schools* (monetary damages)
1994	Equity in Athletics Disclosure Act (EADA)
2005	*Jackson v. Birmingham Board of Education* (retaliation claims)

FIGURE 4.3 *Key Legal Developments*

- 2010 Athletics
- 2010 Harassment and Bullying
- 2011 Sexual Harassment/Violence (Rescinded 2017)
- 2014 Sexual Harassment/Violence, Gender Identity (additional guidance) (Rescinded 2017) (New regulations issued via DOE, effective August 2020)
- 2015 Title IX Coordinators
- 2016 Gender Identity and Transgender (Rescinded 2017) (Reinstated 2021 via Executive Order)

FIGURE 4.4 *OCR Dear Colleague Letters*

NIL and Title IX

As discussed in Chapter 3, recent changes in law and policy allow college athletes to earn income from their names, images, and likenesses (NILs). This is a potential Title IX issue for colleges and universities that circumvent their athletic compliance obligations through third parties, resulting in greater benefits for male athletes. For example, schools must continue to abide by Title IX treatment regulations in areas of publicity and promotion of male and female athletes. Less favorable treatment of female athletes in those areas will impact individual brand-building and reduce NIL opportunities for female athletes. In addition, schools may not recruit male athletes by facilitating NIL deals for them without providing the same quality of recruitment and assistance for female athletes.

Sexual Harassment and Sexual Assault

Sexual harassment and other forms of sexual misconduct in educational institutions also fall under the purview of Title IX. This is because such misconduct, including sexual assault, constitutes a form of sex-based discrimination under the law. The OCR has long recognized sexual harassment in schools as a Title IX issue. The OCR initially issued policy guidance in this area in its Sexual Harassment Guidance, dated March 1997, and revised in 2001. This was intended to clarify the requirements for schools to follow in such cases and applies to students, faculty, and/or staff. Further policy guidance on sexual misconduct was issued under the Obama administration in 2011 and 2014, with detailed reporting and investigation requirements for schools to follow. That OCR guidance was later rescinded by the DOE under the Trump administration. In May 2020, new regulations were released by DOE Secretary DeVos, with a compliance deadline for schools of August 14, 2020. Those regulations narrowed the definition of sexual harassment, added protections for alleged perpetrators, such as the right to cross-examine accusers in live hearings, and discretion for schools to impose a higher standard of proof in sexual assault investigations. Those new regulations are the subject of ongoing litigation and challenges by civil rights groups.

Under the 2020 regulatory changes, the definition of sexual harassment under Title IX involves conduct of a sexual nature that is "severe, pervasive and objectively offensive" so as to affect a student's education or create a hostile work environment for staff members at educational institutions. Reports of sexual assault, dating violence, domestic violence, and stalking do not need to meet the severe, pervasive, and objectively offensive standard. Sexual harassment in the workplace is also governed by a separate law—Title VII—discussed in Chapter 5, Employment Law and Diversity in Sport Organizations. The societal problem of sexual harassment and sexual violence is, of course, widespread beyond athletics; however, it is an important issue in sport law and policy due to the high incidence of cases involving student-athletes as alleged perpetrators, as well as the significant numbers of student-athletes who have been victims in schools and universities. These cases may involve male or female student-athletes, coaches, and/or athletic staff who are alleged perpetrators or alleged victims. It can also arise from same-sex harassment or sexual assault in educational or school sport settings. Sexual misconduct in these forms violate Title IX. Schools are required to investigate such complaints, as they constitute school conduct policy violations. Depending upon the nature of the allegations, these cases might also involve criminal misconduct for which charges may be filed with state and local authorities. Many of these cases gained considerable media attention, as they involved high-profile student-athletes or major universities. In several notable scandals, there were cover-ups by athletic departments and university personnel who, at the expense of victims, sought to protect their star athletes, lucrative athletic programs, and university reputation, by not reporting or properly investigating sexual misconduct claims, in violation of Title IX.

Sexual harassment or assault victims may choose to pursue criminal charges against the alleged perpetrator and/or sue them directly for money damages in a civil action. Under Title IX, however, it is the educational institutions themselves that are subject to potential civil legal liability, including money damages, in these circumstances. This is because under Title IX, it is the duty of schools and institutions to maintain Title IX sexual misconduct policies, identify mandatory reporters, and promptly investigate all complaints. They must also take prompt remedial action, in the form of interim measures and/or discipline, up to and including expulsion, in cases where it is determined that Title IX sexual misconduct policy violations occurred. The applicable regulations and legal interpretations of Title IX by the U.S. Supreme Court provide that a school must not act with "deliberate indifference" in failing to investigate or take prompt remedial action. (See *Gebser v. Lago Vista Independent School District*, 1998.) Schools must accordingly take required steps to ensure a safe environment which does not interfere with educational benefits and is nondiscriminatory based on sex.

Sexual Harassment and Sexual Assault Case Examples

Many schools and universities have faced legal liability as a result of sexual misconduct involving student-athletes or athletic department personnel as alleged perpetrators. Under Title IX, schools must fully investigate internal complaints and take prompt remedial action if sexual misconduct violations are determined to have occurred. This was the fact pattern in the *Franklin* case, noted earlier, in which the U.S. Supreme Court ruled for the first time that money damages were available to a successful Title IX plaintiff. In *Franklin*, a high school teacher and coach sexually harassed and assaulted a 10th-grade student. The student reported this to teachers and school district administrators; however, there was minimal investigation and the student was also pressured by school personnel to refrain from filing charges. The teacher was allowed to resign, and the investigation was closed. The plaintiff later sued the school district under Title IX, seeking money damages for emotional harm and trauma, and the case was decided in her favor.

There is a long list of schools and universities that sought to cover up sexual misconduct that occurred in high-profile athletic programs, or other educational settings. Often, the motivation is to protect star athletes from discipline or to protect the institution's "brand" or reputation. As in *Franklin*, these cases present Title IX issues because schools may be liable for money damages for their failure to investigate and/or take appropriate action for sexual misconduct policy violations. Recently, reported scandals of this nature have occurred at many prominent universities including Baylor University (Baylor), Michigan State University (MSU), The Ohio State University (Ohio State), and University of Michigan (Michigan). An overview of the Title IX allegations in those cases is set forth below.

At Baylor, in a Title IX lawsuit filed in 2017, female student victims alleged that at least 31 of the football team's players committed 52 sexual assaults between the years 2011 and 2014. It was alleged that the head football coach failed to report his knowledge after being made aware of such instances, and the school failed to properly investigate the claims. Regardless of any criminal charges with local authorities, Baylor had a duty under Title IX to investigate and take prompt remedial action, and failed to do so, for which money damages are recoverable.

At MSU, Ohio State, and Michigan, the reported scandals arose from team doctors who allegedly sexually abused student-athletes, with hundreds of victims, male and female, at each of the three universities. In the resulting Title IX lawsuits against MSU, it was alleged that the school failed to investigate or take any remedial action when multiple instances of sexual misconduct on the part of the team physician had been reported to athletic department personnel. In that case, the university was sued on multiple legal theories, but it had substantial liability exposure under Title IX, which led to a reported settlement with many victims, totaling $500 million. At Ohio State and Michigan, the alleged sexual assaults occurred many years ago and the alleged perpetrators are deceased. Those schools have denied specific knowledge of the assaults at the time they occurred, but in Title IX lawsuits filed decades after the alleged assaults, the schools have engaged in negotiations with alleged survivors to pay them monetary settlements in exchange for the dismissal of litigation.

The above cases stand out because of the horrific patterns of abuse, number of assaults, allegations of institutional negligence, criminal charges, and magnitude of the financial settlements paid to survivors. Yet, over many years, Title IX cases of this nature have been filed against many schools and institutions across the country, some involving just one victim who was sexually assaulted by a student-athlete. The schools faced civil liability under Title IX when they failed to investigate the assault or showed deliberate indifference. Examples of these types of cases with plaintiffs receiving favorable settlements after suing their schools include *Simpson v. University of Colorado,* 2005 ($2.5 million settlement for sexual assaults committed by football recruits); *J.K. v. Arizona State University,* 2009 ($850,000 settlement for rape committed by football player); and *Kinsman v. Florida State University,* 2016 ($950,000 settlement for alleged sexual assault by star quarterback).

NCAA Role and Authority

There is much confusion regarding the NCAA's role or enforcement power with respect to Title IX. In fact, the NCAA is not responsible for Title IX enforcement with respect to either athletic compliance or sexual assault. To clarify, Title IX is a federal law under the enforcement of the OCR, a federal agency. Title IX can also be enforced through the federal courts by individuals who elect to file lawsuits against their educational institutions. The NCAA has no formal role with regard to athletic compliance enforcement at its member institutions, and discipline for sexual assault involving student-athletes is not specifically addressed in the NCAA Bylaws.

As discussed earlier in this chapter, the NCAA initially opposed Title IX's application to college athletics at a time when women's athletics had its own governing body, known as the AIAW. After assuming governance over women's programs in the 1980s, the NCAA eventually adopted gender equity principles and best practices in athletics as part of its overall stated mission. As to sexual assault, the NCAA has only recently developed policies applicable to sexual assault prevention and education in its member institutions, and the NCAA's lack of disciplinary action toward schools in instances involving sexual misconduct has been widely criticized.

It was not until August 2017 that the NCAA board of governors developed a sexual assault prevention policy requiring mandatory annual sexual assault prevention education for student-athletes, which school officials must certify is conducted each year. Yet, there is ongoing controversy over student-athletes accused of sexual misconduct continuing to play for their school teams or being permitted to transfer to play elsewhere and avoid a Title IX proceeding. In May 2020, the NCAA addressed this by adopting a rule that requires recruits, transfer athletes, and current athletes to disclose whether they have been accused of a sexual assault that resulted in an investigation or discipline, in either a Title IX proceeding or a criminal case. Many view this recent rule as wholly ineffective because there are no meaningful penalties imposed for violations. A few athletic conferences and individual schools have taken stronger action by banning athletes from intercollegiate competition if they were found to have committed sexual assault. To date, however, the NCAA has not adopted any rule or policy that would effectuate such a ban. This is also a legal issue raised by sexual assault victims, who claim the NCAA failed to supervise, regulate, and monitor its member institutions regarding sexual assaults by student-athletes, or enact appropriate rules designed to minimize the risk of such assaults.

Setting a Precedent

- *Biediger v. Quinnipiac University*
- *Boucher v. Syracuse University*
- *Cannon v. University of Chicago*
- *Cohen v. Brown University*
- *Franklin v. Gwinnett County Public Schools*
- *Gebser v. Lago Vista Independent School District*
- *Jackson v. Birmingham Board of Education*
- *Mayerova v. Eastern Michigan University*
- *Mercer v. Duke University*
- *Pederson v. Louisiana State University*

II. The Ethics

Case Scenarios

Case 1: *To save money, a college athletic department decided to cut two varsity teams: women's volleyball and men's golf. The women's team had 12 scholarships and 18 players on the team roster. The men's team had 4.5 scholarships and a roster of 10. Realizing that they might face a Title IX lawsuit due to the reduced participation opportunities for women, the athletic department decided to elevate an existing women's cheerleading squad to varsity status, and then counted the 24 squad members as female "athletics participants" in their federal reporting obligations under the EADA. Cheerleading is not recognized as a varsity sport by the NCAA. By counting the 24 women, the school asserted it was in Title IX compliance because it now satisfied substantial proportionality under prong one of the three-prong participation compliance test. The college was aware that it could not meet the standards under prongs two or three because it had just eliminated a viable existing women's team.*

Case 1 is a hypothetical drawn from facts presented in prior Title IX lawsuits. It helps illustrate ethical choices made by athletic directors who prioritized saving money over providing meaningful sport participation opportunities for women, as intended by Title IX. To accomplish these ends, the decision-makers circumvented the applicable athletics regulations, in this example, by falsely designating a cheerleading squad as a sport and counting its members as participants. While competitive cheer, under appropriate circumstances, might qualify as a sport, it is not yet so designated by the NCAA, and the OCR has taken the position that cheerleading squads are typically support services, not varsity programs. Further, "athletics participants" under the regulations must receive the same institutionally sponsored support provided to athletes at the school, including coaching, equipment, medical care, training room services, regular practice, and team meetings. The mere designation of a club or team as "varsity" is not enough.

Some schools have been exposed for using these or other deceptive tactics to circumvent Title IX. For example, they manipulate data by artificially inflating or deflating the participation numbers for its male and female athletes. They have accomplished this under the guise of roster management—assigning a fixed roster number target for each men's and women's sport. Roster management can be legitimate if administered openly and fairly, with appropriate target goals consistent with the nature of the sport. But it is a disfavored practice to achieve equity under Title IX because it can be artificially applied, and often is, when there is a lack of qualified female athletes to fill the designated roster slots. Even more brazen, in schools with limited participation opportunities for women, a school might manipulate the data by reporting high numbers for certain women's teams on the first day of competition (the OCR's relevant date for counting participants) and then immediately cut substantial numbers of women from those teams after they were officially "counted" for Title IX compliance purposes. This unethical practice has occurred in schools that use sports such as rowing, track and field, and cross-country to "stuff" or "pad" their numbers, because those teams typically carry large rosters for women. Similarly, a school might mirror this practice to favor men, by under-counting its male athletes on the first day of competition and then adding male athletes to the team's squad list immediately thereafter. In these situations, it is an obvious "red flag" to the OCR when a team is composed of 120 rowers or 150 track athletes, many of whom were permitted to merely sign up without the ability or interest to compete in the first place. Schools cannot fully support such large teams in a manner consistent with Title IX regulations, and these actions subvert the spirit of the law.

Are such practices ever ethically justified? Some argue that athletic directors are under tremendous pressure from their administration with respect to their athletics budget, which must take priority over equity concerns. Or it is asserted that merely "fudging" numbers for reporting purposes is not engaging in any serious discriminatory practices. Another explanation is that, as long as policy enforcement of Title IX remains weak, some athletic directors simply believe they will not get caught and, if they are, there will not be significant consequences for themselves or their school. Finally, this may be another example of decision-making where it is believed that the ends justify the means. This is because many athletic departments view Title IX requirements as unduly burdensome and threatening to their traditionally popular men's programs. In that vein, they see compliance as an obstacle, and are willing to rationalize their actions by maintaining that full compliance with the regulations is not feasible or practical. They are willing to take actions that violate the law rather than impose cost-cutting measures that might jeopardize major men's programs, such as football.

The ethical choices made in these examples are problematic. When saving money is valued over fairness and civil rights, the underrepresented sex is harmed and marginalized. When participation data is manipulated, it is not an insignificant "fudging" of numbers, it violates basic principles of honesty and integrity. The conduct does not become ethically right because of a belief that you will "get away with it" due to lax enforcement of the law. Finally, these decisions and efforts to circumvent Title IX, although incremental at first, are often a slippery slope to more overt sexism and discriminatory practices.

Case 2: *A high school allowed two transgender (male to female) student-athletes to compete on the girl's track team. They frequently outperformed their competitors, winning a combined 15 girls state indoor or outdoor championship events in the last two years. Three biological female high school athletes sued their school districts, claiming that the policy allowing transgender athletes on girls' teams violated Title IX because athletes that were born male had an unfair competitive advantage, and denied those who were born female the opportunities to be successful in their sport and harmed their chances to earn college scholarships.*

Case 2 sets forth key facts that gave rise to a recent Title IX lawsuit filed in the state of Connecticut against the Connecticut Interscholastic Athletic Conference and various public school boards of education. In April 2021, that case was dismissed by a federal judge on procedural grounds after the transgender athletes graduated (Riley, 2021). The legal outcome of cases like this will depend on the court's interpretation of whether "sex" under Title IX includes transgender and gender identity. The state law at issue in Connecticut (Public Act No. 11-55 2011) prohibited discrimination on the basis of gender identity or expression. In addition, their state athletic association policy expressed a commitment to providing transgender student-athletes with equal opportunity to participate in athletic programs consistent with their gender identity. The OCR found that the school's practice in Connecticut violated Title IX.

Participation opportunities for transgender athletes vary greatly depending on the state, sport, athletic association, school district, sport organization, and level of play involved. There are many different laws, policies, and ethical considerations that have impacted the treatment of transgender athletes. Across the country, state legislatures and high school athletic associations have grappled with these questions, particularly as they relate to transgender women and girls. On the one hand, it is argued that biological differences between men and women, including higher testosterone levels in men, give them a natural advantage over women in sports involving speed, strength, and endurance. Many state high school athletic associations have adopted that view and enacted policies providing that participation in high school athletics should be determined by the gender indicated on the athlete's birth certificate. (See, e.g., Alabama High School Athletic Association.) On the other hand, some believe that civil rights protections and inclusive policies should be applied for transgender athletes. Similar to Connecticut in the case example above, states and athletic associations adopting that view have enacted laws and policies providing that all students should have the opportunity to participate in a manner consistent with their gender identity, irrespective of the gender listed on their birth certificate. (See, e.g., California Interscholastic Federation.) Some states take a middle ground with policy restrictions for male to female transgender athletes, requiring medical hormone intervention and a 1-year wait period before allowing them to compete on a women's team. In 2011, the NCAA implemented policies consistent with the middle-ground view with respect to transgender participation in intercollegiate athletics (NCAA Inclusion of Transgender Student-Athletes, 2011). In 2022, amid much political debate and a controversy involving transgender female participation in college women's swimming, the NCAA enacted a new policy in which eligibility requirements for transgender athletes shall be determined by each sport's national governing body. This supplanted the organization's previous policy that was uniform across all sports and based on medical hormone therapy requirements for male to female transgender athletes.

There is ongoing legal debate on this topic, and transgender participation in sport has become a politically divisive issue. As federal and state laws remain unsettled on protections for transgender athletes, there are important ethical considerations at stake which are often at odds. If transgender females are proven to have a competitive advantage, is it fair to allow them on women's teams? Does this undermine the goals of Title IX and sport opportunities for girls and women in sport that were previously limited due to bias and discrimination? Is it condescending to other women athletes to suggest they cannot be successful if transgender participation is allowed, thus reinforcing stereotypes that women are weak and in need of protection? Do you truly promote key virtues in sport, such as equity, fairness, and respect, if you implement policies that disregard the gender identity of student-athletes, or if you act on the disputed belief that gender is exclusively dependent on biology? Do efforts to exclude subsets of women from sport diminish team unity and encourage divisiveness? What about potential emotional harm to trans youth who are excluded from any space or activity? If you assign participation opportunities based on the gender listed on a birth certificate, will it be fair and equitable for transgender males to compete on girls' teams? These ethical questions are complex and not easily answered in terms of what is morally "right" or "wrong." Sport organizations, schools, athletic associations, and administrators increasingly face these ethical choices in their own athletic programs, as transgender rights continue to be the subject of legislative debate and judicial review. It is important to recognize that these ethical choices in sports will potentially influence social change and civil rights for all transgender persons.

Case 3: *You are a high school athletic director. The law in your state provides that girls and women who compete in youth, high school, and college sports may be subject to being challenged by competitors as to their biological sex. If found to not be "female," they would not be able to compete with girls and women. The law states that athletes, if challenged, can verify their sex in one of three ways: a test that confirms their natural hormone levels fall within a certain range, a genetic test that confirms XX chromosomes, or a physical exam to confirm they have female genitals. Your girls' basketball team is in the state finals and the head coach wants to formally dispute the sex of a player on the opposing team. The player is a 17-year-old girl who has been a leading scorer for her team all season and appears to be stronger and more muscular than her teammates. The girl's sex has never been "challenged" before. Your head coach requests your permission to officially file the dispute.*

Case 3 is a hypothetical fact pattern based on a recent Idaho state law called the "Fairness in Women's Sports Act" (Idaho House Bill No. 500, 2020). This law codifies many restrictive policies for transgender athletes, including the requirement that girls who are transgender complete 1 year of hormone therapy as part of gender transition before competing in girls' sports. Similar rules also apply in the NCAA and certain elite international competitions. Significantly, the Idaho law also subjects all female athletes to the possibility of invasive genital and genetic screenings, through its vaguely defined challenge process and stated requirements for "sex verification."

Sex verification or "sex-testing" in sports has a long history and continues to this day in some sport contexts. One of the first mandatory sex tests was issued in 1950. This was implemented for all athletes by the world governing body for track and field known as the International Association of Athletics Federations (IAAF, now known as World Athletics) prior to the European Championships in Belgium. In the 1960s, the testing of female athletes continued due to the widespread suspicion that dominant women athletes from the Soviet Union and Eastern Europe were actually men. In 1968, the Olympic Games officially began sex-testing. Early forms of sex-testing in sport were conducted through physical examinations, specifically of female athletes. Subsequently, chromosome testing was introduced, which was designed to identify biological males who were posing as females. Later, testosterone level testing was implemented to identify female athletes with elevated testosterone levels. This type of testing is still administered today. In 2018, an IAAF rule provided that female athletes competing in certain events (400 m, 800 m, mile, hurdles) were subject to sex verification. The rule stated that female or intersex athletes with testosterone levels equal to or above a certain scientific level (5 nmol/L) cannot compete in those women's events without undergoing hormone treatments that satisfactorily reduce their level for six consecutive months.

The practice of sex verification in all these forms is controversial and has been the subject of many legal challenges. In 1976, Renee Richards successfully sued the United States Tennis Association when she was required to take the "Barr body test" for eligibility to play in the U.S. Women's Open. This was a chromosome test premised on the notion that chromosomes unequivocally determine sex. Richards was a transgender female who had undergone sex reassignment surgery in 1975. Sex reassignment surgery does not change an individual's chromosomes. The court found that Richards was unfairly singled out for the test to exclude her from the competition, in violation of a New York State Human Rights Law (*Richards v. USTA*, 1977). Testosterone level testing has also been legally challenged, most notably in the case of Caster Semenya, a world-champion middle-distance runner from South Africa, who was born and raised female. Semenya is believed to have a condition known as hyperandrogenism, wherein her testosterone levels are naturally elevated, which in her case exceeds the permissible levels under the IAAF rule. For nearly her entire career, Semenya has been forced to undergo this form of sex-verification and periodically has been banned from international competition.

For many reasons, sex-verification is ethically flawed no matter how it is applied or implemented. Physical examinations with genital exams are invasive and humiliating not only for trans, nonbinary, and intersex athletes, but also for cisgender girls. Yet, the Idaho law cited above would allow for such examinations for any high school girl whose sex is challenged prior to competition. Further, chromosome tests clearly confuse biological sex and gender identity. An individual who transitions from male to female, including those who undergo sex reassignment surgery, cannot change their chromosomes, although in all other respects they appear and identify as female. Testosterone level tests arguably present the same ethical flaw. Caster Semenya was born and raised female, but her testosterone level is naturally elevated. Banning her from women's competition sends the message that she is not really a woman due to her natural biological condition. There is also the ethical concern that testosterone level testing may be based on inadequate science, as it is impossible to quantify the level that would tip the scale toward an unfair competitive advantage in certain sports. More broadly, from an ethical standpoint, sex-testing in all these forms is inconsistent with the values of sport and human rights. If a woman is required to undergo medical intervention to compete, athletes like Semenya face risky medical procedures that are intended to undermine their natural talent and abilities. And human rights principles should apply to sport in this context, so that schools and sport organizations are mindful that all individuals are entitled to dignity, respect, and privacy, in addition to applicable legal rights that prohibit discrimination based on sex.

Case 4: *During the period from 2011 to 2014, Baylor University's football program was successful on the field, including a top-25 ranking, Big 12 Conference championship, and elite bowl bid. Football was the highest profile sport at Baylor, with a large fanbase comprising students, alums, and the local community. It was a significant revenue stream for Baylor, and a successful football program led to enhanced financial support from major donors. It was later revealed that during that same time period, at least 31 of the football team's players were alleged to have committed 52 sexual assaults against female students at Baylor. It was alleged that the head football coach failed to report his knowledge after being made aware of several assaults, and that the school failed to properly investigate the claims.*

Case 4 is discussed earlier in this chapter from a legal perspective, as these facts led to numerous Title IX lawsuits against Baylor. But it is also essential to examine the severe ethical failures of coaches, administrators, and university officials at Baylor and other institutions and sport organizations who chose to ignore, disregard, or actively cover up sexual assault and sexual abuse of their students and athletes, and why they did so.

At Baylor, one victim described reporting her claims to the campus police and university health service. She was told by representatives at each location that nothing could be done because the assault occurred off campus. Another victim's mother tried to notify the head football coach and was referred to his secretary, who said they were aware and looking into it. Baylor also had deficient Title IX policies, and procedures and reporting obligations were mishandled by university representatives. During this time, the alleged assaults were not properly investigated, no discipline was issued, and alleged perpetrators continued playing on the team. From an ethical standpoint, the officials who chose to ignore or actively conceal these allegations made a choice to protect the athletes and their school from publicity, civil liability, and criminal charges at the expense of assault victims. They prioritized the benefits to Baylor in terms of financial support and brand recognition that would flow from a successful football program. They unfortunately did so without consideration of the tremendous harm to the women who were assaulted, and they contributed to the unsafe campus environment where more women would likely be victimized (Ethics Unwrapped, 2021). An ethical concept that applies in this scenario is *consequentialism*, which involves judging the morality of acts or decisions based solely on the consequences. In sport, this is sometimes manifested in the value that "winning is everything." Ultimately, in the Baylor case, when the truth emerged publicly following an independent investigation by an outside law firm, the football coach, athletic director, and university chancellor all lost their jobs.

Major sexual assault scandals at other institutions reflect the same ethical failures. In recent lawsuits against Michigan State University, The Ohio State University, and the University of Michigan, it is alleged that various coaches and administrators received reports of sexual assaults of student-athletes by team doctors, yet the reports were not fully investigated at the time and no action was taken against the alleged perpetrators. Due to inaction on the part of these university representatives, the alleged perpetrators continued these assaults over a number of years with impunity. In these cases, the decision-making of those in authority appears to be based on protecting themselves and their school from reputational or financial harm, with little regard for the victims. In these cases, the victims (both male and female) eventually came forward years later with legal claims of institutional negligence and sex discrimination under Title IX.

In addition, U.S. national teams, including USA Gymnastics and USA Swimming, have experienced similar sexual assault scandals involving abuse of their athletes by team personnel, which include allegations of administrative and organizational cover-ups by persons in the highest levels of leadership. The ethical failures in those cases were exposed by the national media and resulted in immediate congressional action with the passage of a federal law known as the Safe Sport Authorization Act of 2017. This law also established the U.S. Center for SafeSport to implement and oversee education and prevention training and enforce the duty to report and safeguard athletes from sexual abuse in amateur sport organizations. In October 2020, Congress built upon the that law with the passage of the Empowering Athletes Act which contains additional safeguards to protect American amateur athletes from sexual, emotional, and physical abuse.

Closing Arguments

Title IX led to major changes in opportunities and resources for girls and women in sport. Those changes would not have occurred without this federal civil rights law that prohibits sex discrimination in educational programs and activities. While the law as applied to athletics has been the subject of controversy, it is clear that its overall impact has been significant and led to a greater acceptance and fairer treatment of women as athletes. Title IX also extends to prohibit sex discrimination at educational institutions in the form of sexual harassment and sexual assault. Enforcement of the law and its policy requirements continues to evolve through our federal courts and agencies today, nearly 50 years after its enactment.

There are also ethical considerations in decision-making that reflect ongoing bias, stereotypes, and sex discrimination in sport. These questionable ethical practices are illustrated in recent scandals at educational institutions and sport organizations, where sport leaders and administrators chose to circumvent athletic compliance regulations or covered up sexual assault and abuse at the expense of the victims. Recent developments in civil rights based on transgender status and gender identity also create ethical dilemmas for sport administrators with respect to the controversial practice of sex verification and the need to create fair opportunities and treatment for transgender athletes.

Study Questions

1. Why does the language of Title IX cover men's and women's athletics programs in schools and universities? Why does Title IX also apply to sexual harassment and sexual assault in educational settings?
2. Do you think that Title IX law and regulations, as applied to athletics, has served its purpose and is therefore no longer necessary?

3. What factors should be evaluated and considered if an athletic program is facing financial difficulties? Is it advisable in such circumstances to cut men's sports or women's sports and, if so, what are the possible ramifications on Title IX athletic compliance?
4. What specific additional roles or measures, if any, should be taken by the NCAA to address the problem of sexual violence that occurs in athletic programs of its member institutions?
5. Discuss the ethical dilemmas posed for an athletic administrator who is asked whether transgender females may participate on the school's girls track team.

Credits

Fig. 4.1: Source: Women's Sports Foundation, "Chasing Equity: The Triumphs, Challenges, and Opportunities in Sports for Girls and Women," *A Women's Sports Foundation Report*, p. 13. Copyright © 2020 by Women's Sports Foundation.

Fig. 4.2: Source: Women's Sports Foundation, "Chasing Equity: The Triumphs, Challenges, and Opportunities in Sports for Girls and Women," *A Women's Sports Foundation Report*, p. 13. Copyright © 2020 by Women's Sports Foundation.

Employment Law and Diversity in Sport Organizations

CHAPTER 5

Opening Statement

Sport organizations and certain professional sports are a workplace. Employment law governs the employment relationship in most workplaces. Teams, leagues, governing bodies, executives, administrators, managers, and athletes might be employers or employees under applicable law. It is essential to know and understand the rights and responsibilities of employers and employees in the workplace as well as the specific federal and state laws that prohibit employment discrimination. The history of these laws is also important because certain prohibited practices were not always illegal. Over many decades, a body of civil rights laws and court interpretations led to the expansion of certain protections for many employees in the workplace.

Section I of this chapter addresses the fundamental legal principles of employment law. It explains the doctrine of "employment at will" and, importantly, the legislative exceptions to that doctrine that have evolved since the 1960s in the form of state and federal civil rights laws. The enactment of the laws and court decisions over several decades have established a body of case law that defines illegal discrimination in the workplace. This includes discrimination based on protected classifications such as race, national origin, religion, sex, age, and disability. There are many sport organizations—professional, intercollegiate, amateur, and youth—that have been the subject of employment discrimination claims. This includes claims related to pay inequity, hiring and firing practices, terms and conditions of employment on and off the playing field, and workplace harassment. To further inform and assist students, this section includes statutory citations, legislative history, and U.S. Supreme Court cases that have influenced and developed this area of the law. Many employment discrimination cases have arisen in sport-related settings, and several of those cases will be examined in detail. Finally, this section sets forth best practices for sport managers to protect against illegal workplace discrimination within their school or sport organization.

LEARNING OBJECTIVES

After reading this chapter, students will:

1. Understand the doctrine of employment at will
2. Know the key federal laws that prohibit discrimination in the workplace
3. Understand the legal remedies and damages for successful plaintiffs in employment discrimination cases
4. Recognize typical fact scenarios that give rise to disparate treatment claims
5. Understand different types of sexual harassment covered under Title VII
6. Consider the ethical implications of diversity, equity, and inclusion initiatives in sport settings

Section II of this chapter addresses the ethical aspects of maintaining a nondiscriminatory sport workplace, and one that values principles of diversity, equity, and inclusion. It examines explicit and implicit bias that has permeated sport organizations, often rooted in negative stereotypes, and reflected in the underrepresentation of women and minorities in coaching and leadership positions. This section also considers the ethical aspects of harassment in sport settings that might not constitute violations of federal or state law, but nonetheless disparages and is dismissive of particular groups of people. Such harassment based on race, ethnicity, religion, national origin, sex, and sexual orientation may show discriminatory intent, and also reflects intolerance and marginalization of those perceived as "others." This is often due to the power imbalance between those in positions of influence in the workplace and those employees who are subordinate. Many sport organizations have addressed these ethical concerns and emphasized corporate social responsibility. This includes proactive measures to implement diversity and inclusion initiatives, together with education, support resources, and sensitivity training for all employees in the workplace.

I. The Law

Employment Law: Fundamentals

Employment at Will Doctrine

Employment at will is a basic doctrine of employment law in the United States. It means generally that an employee can be terminated at any time, for any reason or no reason. However, there are critical exceptions to this doctrine based in contract, public policy, and statutory law. For example, the at-will presumption can be modified by an employment contract that provides for a specific term of employment, or one that allows termination only "for cause" as set forth in the agreement. There are also recognized public policy exceptions to at-will employment, for example, precluding an employer from terminating an employee in retaliation for exercising a legal right such as filing a worker's compensation claim. In addition to these common law exceptions to at-will employment, there are important federal and state antidiscrimination laws that prohibit certain forms of discrimination in the workplace, such as employment actions based upon protected classifications such as race, color, sex, religion, national origin, age, and disability. The subsections below specifically address the federal civil rights statutes that prohibit these forms of illegal discrimination in the workplace and include relevant cases that have arisen under these laws in the sport industry.

Equal Pay Act of 1963 (EPA)

The Equal Pay Act of 1963 (EPA) is a federal statute that amends the Fair Labor Standards Act (FLSA) and is designed to abolish wage disparities based on sex (29 U.S.C. 206(d)).

Legislative History

The EPA was signed into law in June 1963, by President John F. Kennedy, as part of his New Frontier Program. The law prohibits employers from discrimination against employees by paying wages less than those paid to employees of the opposite sex for "equal work on jobs the performance of which requires equal skill, effort, and responsibility, and which are performed under similar working conditions." Violations of the EPA are treated as a failure to pay minimum wage or appropriate overtime under the FLSA, subject to the same penalties. The Education Amendments of 1972 amended the EPA to cover executives, administrators, outside salespeople, and professionals, who were originally excluded from the EPA's protections. Under the law, employees may bring a lawsuit against their employer individually and/or on behalf of themselves and other similarly situated employees.

Within the text of the law, Congress included a clear and concise policy statement and briefly described the problems it was intended to remedy. The clear statement of congressional intent and policy guiding the EPA's enactment indicates the congressional desire to fashion a broad remedial framework to protect employees from wage discrimination on the basis of sex. The U.S. Supreme Court has recognized the view that the EPA must be broadly construed to achieve Congress' goal of remedying sex discrimination. Generally, the EPA was enacted out of concern for the historically weaker bargaining position of women. The EPA protects both men and women; however, it is typically women who are paid less than men. The law was intended to provide a remedy to discriminatory wage structures that reflected outmoded beliefs that men, because of their perceived role in society, should be paid more than women.

Relationship to Title VII and the Ledbetter Act

Wage disparities based on sex for equal work are also prohibited under another civil rights law, Title VII of the Civil Rights Act of 1964 (Title VII), which is addressed further below. Plaintiffs may allege both the EPA and Title VII in cases involving wage inequities based on sex. In 2007, the U.S. Supreme Court restricted the applicable statute of limitations for equal pay claims (*Ledbetter v. Goodyear Tire & Rubber Company*, 2007). Lilly Ledbetter filed suit under Title VII alleging sex discrimination after 19 years of employment at Goodyear, where she consistently received lower performance evaluations and low pay increases compared to her male peers. The plaintiff introduced evidence that, during the course of her employment, several supervisors had given her poor evaluations because of her sex, that as a result of these evaluations her pay was not increased as much as it would have been if she had been evaluated fairly, and that these past pay decisions continued to affect the amount of her pay throughout her employment. Toward the end of her time with Goodyear, she was being paid significantly less than any of her male colleagues. The Supreme Court ruled that Ledbetter's claim was time-barred by Title VII's 180-day limitations period. However, in January 2009, President Obama signed into law the Lilly Ledbetter Fair Pay Act of 2009 (Ledbetter Act), which overturned the Court's holding in *Ledbetter*. This bill, providing that each gender-unequal paycheck is a new violation of the law, was the first bill signed by President Obama. The Ledbetter Act amends Title VII, holding that the 180-day statute of limitations for filing an equal-pay lawsuit regarding pay discrimination resets with each new paycheck affected by that discriminatory action.

EPA—Elements and Defenses

To assert an EPA claim, it is necessary to first satisfy the above-stated elements; that is, that the jobs themselves require the same skill, effort, and responsibilities, and are performed under similar working conditions within the same organization. Thus, regardless of the job title, the two jobs are substantially equal, yet one employee is paid more because of their sex. The burden then shifts to the employer to demonstrate that they are not engaging in illegal discrimination based on sex. The EPA sets forth defenses that an employer has in response to an EPA claim. The law delineates four exceptions for wages that are paid pursuant to (a) a seniority system; (b) a merit system; (c) a system which measures earnings by quantity or quality of production; or (d) a differential based on any factor other than sex. The "factor other than sex" exception has been criticized as a catchall for employers to assert that they have some legitimate business reason for the pay disparity, even though that reason may be pretextual. This may also be problematic if the business reason itself, such as prior salary history, is rooted in prior sex discrimination. The EPA also provides that an employer whose wage differential violates the EPA may not resolve the issue by reducing the wage rate of any employee.

The EPA as Applied to Female Coaches and Athletes

The EPA has become yet another battleground in the sport industry, as women athletes, coaches, administrators, and managers seek to rectify years of discriminatory pay practices. In *Stanley v. University of Southern California* (1999), Marianne Stanley, the head coach of the University of Southern California (USC) women's basketball team, sued over her salary, which was only $62,000 per year, compared to the head coach of men's basketball, George Raveling, who was paid well over six figures. Before her contract expired in 1993, Coach Stanley attempted to negotiate a new contract with USC, seeking the same pay as her male counterpart, but to no avail. After her coaching contract expired, USC revoked its previous offers and began the hiring process for a new coach. Stanley then sued USC for violation of the EPA, Title IX, and retaliatory discharge, among other claims. USC moved for summary judgment on Stanley's claims, alleging she could not show a genuine issue of material fact. The district court granted USC's motion for summary judgment and the Court of Appeals for the Ninth Circuit affirmed, holding that because the pay differential was based on a factor other than sex, USC did not violate the Equal Pay Act or Title IX.

In *Stanley,* the Court found that while the men and women's coaching jobs had the same basic responsibilities with regards to administering the basketball programs, the additional responsibilities of the men's coach involving media and promotional activities made the two jobs substantially different. In addition, the men's coach bore greater revenue-generating responsibilities, and the men's team in fact generated significantly more revenue than the women's team, which made the two positions substantially different despite the common core of tasks. USC also claimed that the disparity in pay was based on Coach Raveling's superior qualifications and coaching experience, which the Court held was a permissible consideration without violating the EPA, since it demonstrated that the disparity was due to a factor other than sex. Employers may pay employees more for stronger credentials, education, and professional experience without violating the EPA. In that case, the male coach was nationally renowned and generated more revenue for the school. The market for coaches at his level in men's basketball was also noted as sufficient to justify his higher salary.

In a later case brought by the head coach of the women's basketball team at Brooklyn College, the District Court for the Eastern District of New York found that the City University of New York (CUNY), which operated Brooklyn College, had engaged in gender discrimination and retaliation in violation of Title VII and the EPA, and that such violations were willful (*Perdue v. City University of New York*, 1998). Molly Perdue, the former women's basketball coach and women's sports administrator at Brooklyn College, sued Brooklyn College, CUNY, and other individually named defendants, alleging gender discrimination and retaliation in violation of Title VII and the EPA. The federal district court upheld the jury's verdict on the EPA claim and the intentional discrimination claim, finding that not only had the defendants violated Title VII and the EPA, but that the EPA violation was willful, entitling her to liquidated damages under the EPA. The Court also found the jury's award of $85,000 in compensatory damages was reasonable, and ordered $134,829 in back wages, $5,262 in unpaid retirement benefits, and $134,829 in liquidated damages, in addition to the $85,000 in compensatory damages, for a total of $359,920, plus prejudgment interest and attorney fees and costs.

In *Perdue*, the Court agreed with the jury's finding that the plaintiff's work required the same skill, responsibility, and effort as the men's basketball coach and men's sports administrator. The Court found that she performed similar work to both of her male counterparts, but for less pay. Regarding her responsibilities as head coach, she and the head coach for men's basketball coached during the same season, number of games, number of players, and number of practices, and they each managed the recruiting, budgets, scholarships, games, and assistant coaches for their respective teams. The plaintiff also performed the same duties as the men's sports administrator, as both were responsible for the daily operation and organization of their programs. CUNY was therefore in violation of the EPA because the plaintiff performed equal work on jobs requiring equal skill, effort, and responsibility as her male counterparts but for less pay, and CUNY could not demonstrate an affirmative defense that the pay differential was based on a factor other than sex. Because the jury found that the EPA violation was willful, the Court ordered liquidated damages in an amount twice that of the back pay awarded. A violation of the EPA is considered willful if the employer either knew or showed reckless disregard for the matter of whether its conduct was prohibited by statute.

More recently, the issue of pay disparity for female athletes has gained a lot of attention with the filing of a lawsuit by players on the highly successful United States Women's National Team (USWNT) (*Morgan v. United States Soccer Federation, Inc.*, 2020). USWNT player Alex Morgan and her teammates sued the United States Soccer Federation (USSF) for alleged violation of both the EPA and Title VII. The plaintiffs contended that they were paid less than their male counterparts on the United States Men's National Team (USMNT) despite having greater success on the field. Both parties moved for summary judgment. The Court held that the professional women soccer players were not paid less than the professional men soccer players, as required to prevail on the wage discrimination claim under the EPA.

Under the EPA, the players had the burden of showing that they performed substantially equal work as the male players, under similar working conditions, and the male players were paid more. The court found that the plaintiffs did not satisfy the third element, since the two teams had different collective bargaining agreements (CBAs), which were negotiated by different unions. Both CBAs contained different systems of incentives, rewards, and bonuses. The plaintiffs pointed out that the game bonus provisions in the women's agreement were substantially less than that of the men's agreement. They also contended that the women players would have received more under the men's agreement over the past few years than they did under their own agreement.

The court rejected both these arguments, holding that while the women's agreement provides for lower game bonuses, finding an EPA violation based on this ignores other benefits received by USWNT players, such as guaranteed annual salaries and severance pay—benefits that USMNT players do not receive. The Court also rejected the argument that the USWNT would have been paid more under the terms of the USMNT's CBA. It noted that the plaintiffs cannot now retroactively deem their CBA worse than the men's CBA by reference to what they would have made had they been paid under the men's pay-to-play terms structure, when they themselves rejected such a structure. Ultimately, the court found that the women's team made more money than the men's team. The women played a total of 111 games and made $24.5 million, averaging $220,639 per game, while the men played 87 total games and made $18.5 million, averaging $212,639 per game. Because the evidence showed that the USWNT played more games and made more money than the USMNT on both a cumulative and an average per-game basis, they failed to demonstrate a triable issue that they were paid less than the USMNT.

In addition, the plaintiffs alleged non-compensation Title VII violations (see below), due to differences based on sex in working conditions, such as the type of playing surface, travel conditions such as the use of chartered flights, and personnel and support services. The court denied the field condition claims but held that the claims for travel conditions and support services could go to trial. In December 2020, the parties voluntarily settled the Title VII claims, which included the USSF's agreement to implement revised polices on four working conditions: charter flights, venue selection, professional support, and hotel accommodations. The settlement, approved by the Court in April 2021, did not address or resolve the pay inequity claims under the EPA, which were previously dismissed by the Court and thereafter appealed by the USWNT. The CBA between the USWNT and USSF expired at the end of 2021, which opened the door for further negotiations in lieu of protracted litigation. In February 2022, the case concluded with a settlement that included U.S. Soccer's payment of $24 million to be divided among the plaintiffs. U.S. Soccer also pledged, as part of the settlement, to equalize pay between the men's and women's teams in all competitions in the next respective collective bargaining agreements (Das, 2022).

Title VII of the Civil Rights Act of 1964 (Title VII)

Title VII of the Civil Rights Act of 1964 (Title VII) is the portion of the landmark Civil Rights Act that prohibits discrimination in employment based on five protected categories: race, color, sex, religion, or national origin (42 U.S.C. § 2000e-2(a)).

Legislative History

In June 1963, President Kennedy gave several speeches calling for the passage of a sweeping civil rights bill in response to continued racial segregation and discrimination, which would address voting rights, public accommodations, and discrimination in employment and education. President Kennedy reminded Americans of the "democratic principle that no man should be denied employment commensurate with his abilities because of his race or creed or ancestry." The bill, as presented to Congress, made no mention of sex discrimination.

The proposed bill, which President Kennedy called the "Civil Rights Act," (the "Act") was opposed by many in Congress, including those who saw the bill as an intrusion on states' rights. President Kennedy was assassinated before he could see the bill passed into law, but his successor, President Lyndon B. Johnson, made passage of the Act a priority upon assuming office. Just five days after President Kennedy's assassination, President Johnson gave a speech to Congress vowing to continue President Kennedy's fight to ensure passage of the Act, seeking quick action on the bill from Congress. In an attempt to derail the bill, Congressman Smith of Virginia offered an amendment to the House version of the bill to insert "sex" after the word "religion" as a protected classification from employment discrimination, a somewhat shocking notion at that time due to the generally accepted practices that favored men in the workplace. Nevertheless, the House passed the bill as amended, and President Johnson signed the bill into law in July 1964.

The Act was originally designed to integrate African Americans into the mainstream of society by protecting voting rights, requiring desegregation in places of public accommodation and education, and prohibiting employment discrimination. Today, the Act has broad significance for all racial and ethnic minorities, religious organizations, women, and the entire LGBTQIAP community.

Unlawful Employment Practices Under Title VII

Title VII makes it unlawful for an employer to fail or refuse to hire or to discharge any individual, or otherwise to discriminate against any individual with respect to that individual's compensation, terms, conditions, or privileges of employment. Title VII also makes it unlawful to limit, segregate, or classify employees or applicants for employment in any way that would deprive any individual of employment opportunities or otherwise adversely affect the employee's status as an employee, because of such individual's race, color, religion, sex, or national origin (Id. at § 2000e-2(b)). Similar prohibitions apply to labor organizations and training programs, such as apprenticeships. Title VII also prohibits discriminatory employment practices that have a disparate impact on individuals of a particular race, color, sex, religion, or national origin when the challenged practice is not job related for the position in question or consistent with business necessity.

Title VII provides an exception to its antidiscrimination provisions "where religion, sex, or national origin is a bona fide occupational qualification" reasonably necessary to the normal operation of a particular business or enterprise. This is known as the "BFOQ defense." Race is not considered a BFOQ; however, in rare circumstances gender may be, for example, requiring that a female be hired for the job of a women's restroom attendant. The BFOQ defense was set forth by the restaurant chain Hooters of America when it was sued by a class of men for failure to hire them as servers. In that case, Hooters of America argued that the hiring of females only as servers is reasonably necessary to the operation of its business model under the BFOQ defense. Nevertheless, Hooters of America quickly settled the lawsuit in a confidential settlement and had previously settled a similar class action lawsuit in 1997 for $3.5 million. Hooters of America continues to only hire female servers (See *Grushevski v. Texas Wings Inc.*, 2009). Title VII also permits educational institutions to hire and employ employees of a particular religion if the educational institution is, in whole or substantial part, owned, supported, controlled, or managed by a particular religion or religious corporation or association, or if the curriculum of the educational institution "is directed toward the propagation of a particular religion."

An individual wishing to challenge an employment practice under Title VII must first file a charge with the federal agency called the Equal Employment Opportunity Commission (EEOC). The EEOC is the federal agency responsible for implementing and investigating violations of Title VII and other civil rights statutes. Such a charge must be filed within a specified period (either 180 or 300 days, depending on state law) after the alleged unlawful employment practice occurred, and if the employee does not submit a timely EEOC charge, the employee may not challenge that practice in court.

In addition to prohibiting discrimination, Title VII also prohibits retaliation against those who oppose any unlawful employment practice under the statute, or because someone has made a charge, testified, assisted, or participated in any manner in an investigation, proceeding, or hearing, which is generally understood to be "protected activity." During fiscal year 2019, the EEOC received more charges alleging unlawful retaliation after engaging in protected activity to oppose unlawful employment practices than it had received charges alleging discriminatory employment practices. This has been a trend in EEOC filings since 2012.

Applicability of Title VII to Sport

Title VII defines an employer as "a person engaged in an industry affecting commerce who has fifteen or more employees for each working day in each of twenty or more calendar weeks in the current or preceding calendar year, and any agent of such a person." Thus, Title VII has a broad reach, encompassing most employers, even smaller entities. The term "person" includes one or more individuals, governments, governmental agencies, political subdivisions, labor unions, partnerships, associations, corporations, legal representatives, mutual companies, joint-stock companies, trusts, unincorporated organizations, trustees, trustees in cases under title 11, or receivers. Under Title VII, an employee is an individual "employed by an employer," thus, independent contractors are excluded from the Act's protections. In Title VII employment discrimination cases, a burden-shifting framework applies. First, the employee makes a prima facie case of discrimination by proving they are a member of a protected class and treated differently than other similarly situated employees because of that classification. Next, the employer is afforded the opportunity to provide a legitimate nondiscriminatory reason for its employment actions. Finally, if the employer makes that showing, the burden shifts back to the employee to demonstrate that the employer's reason is merely a pretext for unlawful discrimination.

There have been many Title VII claims against sport organizations, college athletic departments, and professional sport leagues filed by employees who alleged that they suffered adverse employment actions based on their protected classification (race, color, national origin, religion, and/or sex). For example, a successful Title VII case was brought against the National Basketball Association (NBA) when the league refused to hire a qualified woman as a referee. The NBA was unable to present a viable legal defense for its rule that precluded women from referee jobs in the league. After a six-day jury trial, the NBA was found liable for intentional discrimination based on sex under Title VII. The jury awarded the plaintiff $100,000 in lost wages, $750,000 for emotional distress, and $7,000,000 in punitive damages (*Ortiz-Del Valle v. National Basketball Association*, 1999). In intercollegiate athletics, a Title VII case was filed by a highly qualified male applicant for a head coaching position for women's crew at the University of Pennsylvania. He sued the university when he was not offered an interview for the job. The school hired a woman instead, who was allegedly less qualified. The federal court jury found that the school's failure to interview the plaintiff for the job was sex discrimination under Title VII. The jury awarded the plaintiff $115,000 in damages, which was upheld by the Third Circuit on appeal (*Medcalf v. Trustees of the University of Pennsylvania*, 2003). In 2017, another professional sport league, Major League Baseball (MLB), was named as a defendant in a Title VII lawsuit. In that case, the plaintiff was umpire Angel Hernandez, who alleged discrimination in the manner in which MLB's promotion and postseason assignment policies for umpires were administered. Hernandez claimed that despite his excellent accuracy rating on calling balls and strikes in 2016, he was not assigned to work any of the World Series games and entered the 2017 season with the same job title he had when he began working for MLB more than 20 years prior. The plaintiff alleged that he was a member of a protected class under Title VII based on his Latino ethnicity, the color of his skin, and his Cuba-born national origin. He claimed that he was passed over for promotion and excluded from working the World Series while other less-experienced, lower-rated umpires outside of his protected class were promoted to such prestigious positions. The MLB argued that Hernandez had not demonstrated the necessary leadership ability and situational management skills in critical high-pressure roles on a consistent basis, and that was the basis for its assignment decision. In March 2021, the federal district court granted MLB's motion for summary judgment, dismissing the Title VII case. The Court found that the MLB did not violate Title VII because it established a clear and specific legitimate nondiscriminatory reason for its actions involving Hernandez, unrelated to the plaintiff's race, color, or national origin (*Hernandez v. The Office of the Commissioner of Baseball and Major League Baseball Blue, Inc.*, 2021).

Sexual Harassment Under Title VII

Sexual harassment is a form of sex discrimination prohibited by Title VII. Title VII makes it unlawful to harass a person, whether an applicant or employee, because of that person's sex. Harassment can include unwelcome sexual advances, sexual comments or derogatory statements based on sex, requests for sexual favors, and other verbal or physical harassment of a sexual nature when submission to such conduct is made either explicitly or implicitly a term or condition of an individual's employment (29 CFR §1604.11(a)(1)). The EEOC guidelines define two types of sexual harassment: "quid pro quo" and "hostile environment." Quid pro quo harassment occurs when submission to or rejection of such conduct by an individual is used as a basis for employment decisions affecting such individual. Hostile environment harassment occurs when such conduct has the purpose or effect of unreasonably interfering with an individual's work performance, or creating an intimidating, hostile, or offensive working environment. Sexual harassment, like all harassment under Title VII, must be severe or pervasive to be legally actionable; isolated or stray comments in the workplace are insufficient to demonstrate a hostile working environment.

Under Title VII, the victim of sexual harassment, as well as the harasser, may be a woman or a man. The victim does not have to be of the opposite sex. Further, the victim does not have to be the person harassed, but could be anyone affected by the offensive conduct. Harassing conduct must be unwelcome, but it can be unwelcome as to a third party observing the behavior, even if the employees engaging in the conduct find it welcome as to each other. The harasser can be the victim's supervisor, an agent of the employer, a supervisor in another area, a co-worker, or a non-employee. Unlawful sexual harassment under Title VII may occur without economic injury to or discharge of the victim.

When the sexual harassment is between fellow employees, an employer is legally responsible where the employer (or its agents or supervisory employees) knows or should have known of the conduct, unless it can show that it took immediate and appropriate corrective action. Similarly, an employer may be legally responsible for the sexually harassing acts of non-employees occurring in the workplace, where the employer (or its agents or supervisory employees) knows or should have known of the conduct and failed to take immediate and appropriate corrective action (29 C.F.R. §1604.11(e)).

An employer is vicariously liable for an actionable hostile work environment created by a supervisor. In those cases in which the employee has suffered no tangible job consequences as result of the supervisor's actions, the employer may raise an affirmative defense to liability or damages, which requires the employer to show that it exercised reasonable care to prevent and correct promptly any sexually harassing behavior, and that the employee unreasonably failed to take advantage of any preventive or corrective opportunities provided or to avoid harm otherwise.

Within the sport industry, not unlike many other corporate and business work environments, sexual harassment claims are prevalent and frequently the subject of public attention. Title VII sexual harassment claims have been filed against players, coaches, and upper management in various sports organizations. A noted example in the NBA occurred within the New York Knicks organization. In 2007, Anucha Browne Sanders, a former executive employee of Madison Square Garden (Garden), sued the Garden, its CEO James L. Dolan, and its former coach and general manager Isiah Thomas for sexual harassment, ultimately winning an $11.6 million jury verdict against the Garden and individual defendant Dolan. The plaintiff claimed that defendant Thomas subjected her to hostility and sexual advances starting in 2004, after he arrived as president for basketball operations, and that her subsequent firing by Dolan and the Garden was in retaliation for her sexual harassment complaint. The Garden opposed the retaliation claim by alleging that the plaintiff was fired for incompetence and for interfering with the investigation of her sexual harassment complaint. The defense attorneys also argued that the plaintiff only raised her claims after she was denied a role overseeing basketball operations and had had several difficult budget meetings with her supervisors, where she did not perform well. After the trial, the jury found in favor of the plaintiff and awarded her $11.6 million in punitive damages. The court scheduled a hearing on an additional $9.6 million in compensatory damages sought by the plaintiff. Three days before that court hearing, the parties agreed to settle the case for $11.5 million.

In 2020, 15 women who were previously employed by the Washington Football Team reported that they were sexually harassed and verbally abused by senior staff in the workplace. Such claims fall under the purview of Title VII, if filed in court. The NFL launched an independent investigation of the allegations. The investigation findings included bullying, intimidation, sexual harassment, and overall lack of respect for women in the workplace environment. In 2021, the NFL imposed a $10 million fine on the Washington team following the results of that investigation.

> **Case Notes:** *Turnbow v. Houston Texans*
>
> This case is one among several NFL cheerleader lawsuits filed against the respective NFL teams, based in part on allegations of employment discrimination based on sex, in violation of Title VII. These cases also involve alleged wage and hour violations under the Fair Labor Standards Act (FLSA) due to the alleged failure to pay the cheerleaders minimum wage and overtime pay. The Title VII claims asserted by the cheerleaders included that they had been subjected to physical assault and abuse by their coach while forced to adhere to strict appearance and private conduct standards that were intrusive, harassing in nature, embarrassing, and discriminatory based on sex. In Turnbow, the federal court litigation was transferred to private arbitration, based on a provision in the employment contracts signed by the cheerleaders, and the outcome is not publicly available. Other NFL teams have chosen to disband or not form a cheerleading team rather than eliminating these discriminatory practices.

Sexual Orientation, Transgender, and Gender Identity Under Title VII

In a recent landmark decision in *Bostock v. Clayton County, Georgia* (2020), the Supreme Court delivered a historic victory for the LGBTQIAP community when it ruled that an employer who discriminates against an employee on the basis of sexual orientation or gender identity violates Title VII. This decision was a consolidation of three cases, *Bostock v. Clayton County*; *Altitude Express, Inc. v. Zarda*; and *R.G. & G.R. Harris Funeral Homes, Inc. v. EEOC*. In each of these cases, an employee was fired shortly after the employee's homosexual or transgender status was revealed.

The underlying facts of the three cases raised similar issues regarding sex discrimination under Title VII. Bostock was a child welfare advocate employed by Clayton County, Georgia. After a decade with the county, he started participating in a gay recreational softball league. Shortly after this, Bostock was fired for conduct "unbecoming" a county employee. Zarda was a skydiving instructor at Altitude Express in New York. He was fired days after mentioning to his employer that he was gay. Stephens worked at R.G. & G.R. Harris Funeral Home in Michigan, presenting as a male when she initially began employment. A couple of years into her employment, Stephens informed her employer that she intended to live and work as a woman after returning from an upcoming vacation. She was fired before she left for the vacation. Each employee sued for a Title VII violation, alleging unlawful discrimination on the basis of sex. The Eleventh Circuit held that Title VII does not prohibit employers from firing employees for being gay and therefore Bostock's claims could be dismissed as a matter of law. The Second and Sixth Circuits, however, allowed the claims of both Zarda and Stephens to proceed, respectively, holding that Title VII prohibits employers from discriminating against an employee on the basis of sexual orientation (*Zarda*) or gender identity (*Stephens*). The U.S. Supreme Court agreed to hear the consolidated cases to resolve the issue of whether Title VII protects against discrimination based on sexual orientation or transgender status.

The Court first examined the ordinary public meaning of the terms in Title VII. It assumed that "sex" referred only to biological distinctions between male and female. Next, it interpreted the phrase "because of" as incorporating the simple and traditional "but for" causation. This form of causation is established when the discrimination would not have happened "but for" the employee's sex. Even if there are multiple but-for causes, so long as the employee's sex is one but-for cause, it is enough to trigger the law. Finally, the Court defined "discriminate" as intentionally treating an individual differently from others who are similarly situated. The focus of Title VII is on individual treatment, not groups. Taken together, an employer violates Title VII when it intentionally fires an individual employee based in part on sex.

The majority opinion of the Court concluded that it is impossible to discriminate against a person for being homosexual or transgender without discriminating against that individual based on sex. The Court considered an example where an employer with two employees, a male and female who are both attracted to men, fires only the male employee because of his sexual orientation. The employer essentially discriminates against the male employee for the same actions or traits it tolerates in its female employees. In such a situation, it is undeniable that the employee's sex plays an "unmistakable" role in the employer's decision to discharge him. In a dissenting opinion, Justice Alito pointed out that both "sexual orientation" and "gender identity" do not appear on the list of protected characteristics in Title VII, noting that proposals to amend the statute to include sexual orientation and gender identity have not been passed. He accused the majority of usurping the legislative role by interpreting Title VII to protect homosexual and transgender people, which Congress never considered in passing the Civil Rights Act of 1964.

As previously discussed in Chapter 4, *Bostock* is particularly important in its potential application to transgender athletes. This is because the case will inform how courts construe Title IX's prohibition on sex-based discrimination in education, including their analyses relating to transgender athletes. In his dissent in *Bostock,* Alito wrote that applying the same Title VII definition of "sex" to Title IX could "undermine one of that law's major achievements, giving young women an equal opportunity to participate in sports." This was already at issue in a Connecticut high school Title IX case just prior to the Bostock decision. In that case, the state high school athletic association (CIAC) policy allowed transgender girls (individuals assigned a male sex at birth but identifying as female) to compete on female athletic teams, resulting in a complaint filed by three cisgender female track athletes, who alleged harm from the presence of two transgender female athletes in their track competition. In May 2020, the OCR issued a Letter of Impending Enforcement Action to the association, claiming the policy discriminates against women in violation of Title IX. The three female athletes who were the complainants to OCR also sued CIAC and the involved school districts, raising the same Title IX claim. The Trump administration filed a statement of interest in that case, asserting that the CIAC's transgender policy was an incorrect interpretation of Title IX. A federal judge dismissed the Connecticut lawsuit in April 2021 as essentially moot, because the transgender athletes who competed had graduated from high school and the plaintiffs could not identify others currently competing.

This reflects the significant political and legal aspects related to the issue of transgender athlete participation in school sports. Under the Obama administration, the DOE policy guidance to schools was to treat transgender students as the gender with which they identify or face sanctions for violating Title IX. The Trump administration rescinded this policy guidance in 2017. In January 2020, immediately upon taking office, President Biden issued an Executive Order that extends protection based on sexual orientation, transgender status, and gender identity in federally funded programs. Executive orders are subject to judicial review and may be overturned if the orders lack support by statute or the Constitution. Based on *Bostock*, the legal argument for transgender inclusion in school sports is that if it is unlawful discrimination to discriminate based on transgender status under Title VII, then the same should be true under Title IX.

Case Notes: *Morgan v. United States Soccer Federation, Inc.*

(Equal Pay Act and Title VII)

This case (discussed in detail earlier in this chapter) is noteworthy as it involves well-known female athletes who happen to be employed by the same organization as their male counterparts. This creates employment law issues not typically found in sport, because the women's team and men's team both "work" for the same employer, in this case the United States Soccer Federation. While there are many historical examples of women athletes being paid less than men (e.g., professional tennis and golf), those examples do not raise employment law claims because the athletes are independent contractors, not employees, and they do not work for a single organization.

In this case, the plaintiffs alleged violation of two different federal laws—the Equal Pay Act (EPA) and Title VII. The EPA claims were based on the argument that the women's team and men's team performed jobs that required the same skill, effort, and responsibilities, under similar working conditions, but the women were paid less. The Court dismissed the EPA claim based on the different pay structures that had been agreed to under the respective men's and women's collective bargaining agreements. The Title VII claims did not involve wages; instead, they related to alleged disparities in working conditions for the men's and women's teams. The Title VII claims were voluntarily resolved between the parties without trial and approved by the Court in April 2021. The wage disparities were the subject of an appeal by the USWNT. In February 2022, the case was settled by U.S. Soccer's $24 million payment to the plaintiffs, together with a pledge to equalize the pay structure in the next men's and women's collective bargaining agreements.

Age Discrimination in Employment Act (ADEA)

Congress did not include age as a protected classification under Title VII of the Civil Rights Act of 1964. Three years later, another federal law was passed to specifically prohibit age discrimination in employment. The Age Discrimination in Employment Act (ADEA) prohibits employment discrimination on the basis of age (29 U.S.C. §§ 621 *et seq.*). It protects persons who are at least 40 years old and applies to businesses with 20 or more employees whose activities involve interstate commerce. If a qualified applicant is age 40 or older, they cannot be discriminated against on the basis of age in hiring and/or firing, promotion, discharge, compensation, or terms, conditions, or privileges of employment. The ADEA is enforced by the EEOC. The ADEA allows for a private cause of action against an employer by the aggrieved individual.

A high-profile age discrimination lawsuit in intercollegiate athletics was filed by a 64-year-old former assistant football coach at the University of Notre Dame (*Moore v. University of Notre Dame*, 1998). In that case, the plaintiff Joseph Moore claimed violation of the ADEA after he was fired by Head Football Coach Bob Davie because, as Davie himself allegedly said, he needed someone younger for the job. The plaintiff had evidence that Davie had discussed the firing with others, including student-athletes, and always referencing the plaintiff's age. Notre Dame offered a defense that there were other reasons for the firing, including "after-acquired" evidence of alleged abuse on the part of the plaintiff. The case went to trial and the jury found in favor of Coach Moore, finding that Notre Dame violated the ADEA. Moore received back pay and liquidated damages because the violation was willful. Post-trial, Moore sought reinstatement to his former coaching position or an award of "front pay" in lieu of reinstatement. The court ruled that reinstatement was inappropriate in the case because there was no available position for his return. The plaintiff was awarded front pay in an amount equal to two years' salary, plus post-judgment interest, and attorney fees.

Americans with Disabilities Act (ADA)

In 1990, Congress passed comprehensive federal legislation to prohibit discrimination against persons with disabilities (42 U.S.C. §§ 12101 et seq.). The ADA defines a covered disability as a physical or mental impairment that "substantially limits" one or more major life activities, a history of having such an impairment, or being regarded as having such an impairment. The EEOC is charged with interpreting the ADA with regard to discrimination in employment. Under various titles, the ADA extends protections to persons with disabilities in employment, state and local government, and places of public accommodation. Unlike Title VII of the Civil Rights Act of 1964, the ADA also requires covered employers to provide reasonable accommodations to employees with disabilities, and imposes accessibility requirements on public accommodations such as restaurants, hotels, theaters, and stadiums.

Applicability of ADA to Sport

Title I of the ADA applies to employment and prohibits discrimination against qualified persons with a disability. To prove a case under Title I, the plaintiff must establish that they have a disability (as defined under the ADA), they are qualified for the job, and were discriminated against because of their disability. Further, under Title I, an employer has a legal duty to provide reasonable accommodations for qualified employees with a disability. This means that an employer must accommodate work-related needs of a disabled employee (e.g., a ramp for a wheelchair-bound employee or an enhanced monitor for a visually impaired employee) to allow them to perform their job, as long as those accommodations do not impose an undue burden on the employer, or fundamentally alter the nature of the job. Title I applies to a wide range of places of employment, which includes sport organizations or sport-related businesses, with 15 or more employees. Title II applies to state and local government, which covers public schools and school districts, including their extracurricular athletic programs.

Title III of the ADA also has been applied in many sport contexts. Title III prohibits disability discrimination in places of public accommodation. This specifically includes recreational facilities, stadiums, arenas, gymnasiums, and golf courses. There are several forms of disability discrimination that fall under Title III, including barring people with disabilities from enjoying goods and services of the place of public accommodation, and failing to make reasonable modifications or remove barriers to access for persons with disabilities. Many universities and professional sport teams have been sued under Title III for failure to provide sufficient disability seating at their stadiums and/or failing to provide reasonable modifications for the disabled with respect to facility parking and access to concessions and restrooms. For example, in 2019, the San Francisco 49ers and City of Santa Clara were defendants in a class action lawsuit filed under Title III of the ADA on behalf of disabled fans of the team who lacked access to Levi's Stadium. The defendants settled the case by agreeing to pay $24 million and make the stadium and its parking lot more accessible to fans in wheelchairs, who alleged that they encountered barriers in buying tickets, parking, reaching their seats, and using the restrooms (*Nevarez et al. v. Forty Niners Football Company, LLC*, 2020).

A well-known Title III case in a professional sport context was brought by a PGA Tour golfer, Casey Martin, who suffered from a rare circulatory disorder that caused a painful muscle and bone condition in his leg, making it difficult for him to walk. He requested that the PGA Tour accommodate his disability by allowing him to use a golf cart in competition. The PGA Tour, however, denied his request for an exception to their "no-cart" rule. Martin then sued the PGA Tour, alleging that the rule failed to make tournaments accessible to disabled persons in violation of Title III of the ADA. Martin's case went all the way to the U.S. Supreme Court, which ruled 7-2 in favor of Martin. The Court found that while the PGA Tour was not Martin's employer under Title I, it was covered under Title III because golf courses are places of public accommodation. As such, the PGA Tour had a duty to provide reasonable accommodations to Martin, who was a qualified individual with a disability. The PGA Tour argued that a golf cart was not a reasonable accommodation because it would give Martin an unfair competitive advantage, and the walking was essential to the rules of golf. The Court found otherwise and ruled that allowing Martin to use a golf cart was a reasonable accommodation because it would not fundamentally alter the rules of the game (*PGA Tour, Inc. v. Martin*, 2001). Some commentators, including dissenting Justice Scalia, expressed policy concerns that this decision would open the door to special rules and unfair treatment in favor of disabled athletes, which was not good for sport. Instead, the aftermath of the Martin case has shown that no such slippery slope occurred, and the integrity of sport was not threatened by giving a disabled athlete the opportunity to compete fairly with reasonable accommodations.

College Athletes as Employees

The definition of "employee" is critically important in intercollegiate sport, as the NCAA, its member institutions, and athletic conferences continue to face employment-related legal claims brought by student-athletes. Those claims are premised on the argument that student-athletes should treated as employees of the colleges or universities for which they play. This is an issue that has been examined in a worker's compensation context (state law) as well as under our federal labor laws related to minimum wage and overtime under the Fair Labor Standards Act (FLSA) and the right to organize as a union under the National Labor Relations Act (NLRA). To date, the efforts to attain employee status have been unsuccessful in areas of worker's compensation law, minimum wage and overtime pay, and the ability to organize as a union, as follows.

Worker's Compensation Law

A college football player was injured while playing football for Western Michigan University. His athletic scholarship was honored for the year following his injury but was then revoked. He sued the university, claiming that he was an employee under the Michigan Worker's Disability Compensation Act, and therefore entitled to rights and benefits of employment, including maintaining his scholarship (*Coleman v. Western Michigan University*, 1983). The court applied a longstanding "economic reality" test to determine whether an employment relationship existed between the student and the school. That test examines four factors: (a) the proposed employer's right to control or dictate the activities of the proposed employee; (b) the proposed employer's right to discipline or fire the proposed employee; (c) the payment of "wages" and, particularly, the extent to which the proposed employee is dependent on the payment of wages or other benefits for his daily living expenses; and, (d) whether the task performed by the proposed employee was an integral part of the proposed employer's business. The court evaluated all of these factors as it related to this scholarship football player. The court found that he fell short in satisfying the fourth element of the test, that is, that playing football, according to the court, was not an integral part of the defendant university's business. Instead, the court found that the business of the university was education, and taking all of these factors into account, the football player was a student-athlete and not an employee. A similar argument was tested in the state of Indiana by a college football player who sought state worker's compensation benefits after he was rendered a quadriplegic during the course of his college football practice. The court found that he was not an employee of the university and therefore not entitled to worker's compensation benefits, which specifically apply to employees who are injured in the scope of their employment (*Rensing v. Indiana State University Board of Trustees*, 1982).

Minimum Wage and Overtime Pay

In 2019, the Court of Appeals for the Ninth Circuit affirmed a district court decision to dismiss a complaint for failure to state a claim, holding that student-athlete football players are not employees of the NCAA or the PAC-12 conference (*Dawson v. National Collegiate Athletic Association*, 2019). The case was originally brought under the Fair Labor Standards Act, which regulates wages and broadly defines "employee," and the California Labor Code. In the complaint, Dawson alleged that the NCAA and the PAC-12 acted as an employer of the student-athlete class members by "prescribing the terms and conditions under which student-athletes perform services." Dawson further claimed that both entities were joint employers who failed to pay wages, including minimum wage and overtime pay, to Dawson and to class members in violation of federal and state labor laws.

The court ruled that neither the NCAA nor the PAC-12 could meet the FLSA's "economic realities" test, because neither entity offered compensation to the players (scholarships were issued by the individual colleges, and the NCAA rules prohibiting compensation beyond scholarships did not create any expectation of compensation), and neither had the ability to hire or fire the players, despite extensive regulation of collegiate sports. Further, the NCAA and PAC-12 regulations were not created in an effort to evade liability under the FLSA, which is the final element of the test. While Dawson argued that the substantial revenues the student-athletes generated for the two entities should alter the economic realities test, the court disagreed, holding that "in the context of our preceding analysis, the revenue generated by college sports does not unilaterally convert the relationship between student-athletes and the NCAA into an employment relationship." The court assessed similar factors provided under the California Labor Code, reaching the same conclusion.

Ability to Organize as a Union

Over the last century, professional athletes have taken advantage of the right to organize as a union, as specified in the National Labor Relations Act enacted in 1935 (NLRA). This legislation provided important rights to American workers, including the right to form, join, or assist labor organizations; the right to bargain collectively with an employer; and the right to engage in concerted activities (29 U.S.C. §157). Notably, players in the four main professional sports leagues—NBA, NFL, MLB, and NHL—all have player unions who collectively bargain with management (owners) for the terms and conditions of employment that are embodied in collective bargaining agreements.

Unions seeking to represent student-athletes have raised similar claims against colleges and universities under the NLRA, alleging that as employees of the educational institution, scholarship athletes have the right to form and join unions to collectively bargain for their terms and conditions of employment. (See, e.g., *Northwestern University and College Athletes Players Association*, 2014.) In 2014, the regional director for Region 13 of the National Labor Relations Board (NLRB) held that scholarship football players of Northwestern University were employees for purposes of collective bargaining and directed the election process to continue. Northwestern University appealed the regional board decision. The decision was overturned by the full NLRB in 2015, which declined to assert jurisdiction over the players, stating that labor stability would not be promoted by its ruling on the issue, noting that any such jurisdiction would only apply to private educational institutions, since the NLRB has no authority over public institutions. In a January 2017 memorandum, the general counsel of the NLRB concluded that the NLRB precedent permitted a finding that Division I Football Bowl Subdivision scholarship football players in private colleges and universities are employees under the NLRA. After the Trump administration appointed the new NLRB General Counsel Peter Robb, he rescinded General Counsel Memorandum 17-01 in one of his first official acts in December 2017. As it stands, the NLRB's decision to decline asserting jurisdiction does not legally preclude a future attempt to unionize by other college athletes.

Setting a Precedent

- *Moore v. University of Notre Dame*
- *Stanley v. University of Southern California*
- *Sanders v. Madison Square Garden, L.P.*
- *Perdue v. City University of New York*
- *Turnbow v. Houston Texans, L.P.*
- *USWNT v. U.S. Soccer Federation*
- *PGA Tour, Inc. v. Martin*
- *Kennedy v. Bremerton School District*
- *Bostock v. Clayton County, Georgia*
- *Dawson v. National Collegiate Athletic Association*

II. The Ethics

Case Scenarios

Case 1: *A new men's professional rugby league (RGB) just completed its inaugural season. The league is composed of 8 teams, with a 14-game season. Each team has a roster of 24 men under individual salaried contracts with their respective teams. To add entertainment value and gain fan and media attention for the new league, RGB held auditions for an all-female cheerleading/dance squad to perform at half-time of each game. The league selected 10 cheerleaders/dancers and paid each of them a nominal contracting fee for the entire season, plus actual expenses. The squad practiced 20 hours per week in addition to performing at the games. They were then featured in skimpy outfits in a provocative RGB calendar and required to sign team rules, which include hair and makeup requirements, individual weigh-ins, and express prohibitions on fraternizing with any RGB players. The RGB players are not subject to a specific code of personal conduct or similar policies. Near the end of the first season, one cheerleader was dismissed from the squad after she complained to the RGB commissioner that she was sexually harassed by an RGB player. RGB also registered federal copyrights on the calendar and its featured photos and sold the calendars online and at games throughout the season, sharing the revenue equally among the RGB team owners.*

Case 1 presents legal issues as well as ethical issues related to discriminatory employment practices, explicit bias, implicit bias, and sex stereotyping in sport. Women cheerleaders and dancers who work for professional sport leagues have often been underpaid, sexually harassed, and hypersexualized or exploited based on gender ideology in sport that considers women to be best suited to roles that support men. The facts are not dissimilar from many NFL cheerleader cases that have alleged sexist and discriminatory work rules and policies, harassment, and disparate treatment based on sex.

As to potential legal claims, under these facts, because the women were hired as independent contractors and not employees, it appears that RGB intentionally circumvented minimum wage and hours laws as well as Title VII. The women are not entitled to minimum wage because, even though they work for the league, they are not legally considered employees of RGB. This also means that the women do not have protections against illegal discrimination based on sex in the workplace under Title VII, including the alleged sexual harassment and apparent retaliatory dismissal for complaining about discrimination. In addition, by obtaining exclusive copyright protection on the calendar and photos, RGB likely would prevail in claims by the individual cheerleaders for compensation for their names and images.

Ethically, it is important to recognize gender ideology as it applies to sport. Gender ideology consists of interrelated ideas and beliefs that are widely used to define masculinity and femininity. Historically, sports have always been male-identified and male-centered, as reflected in sports like football or rugby that involve sometimes violent physical contact, dominance, and conquest. Male-dominated sport organizations have seen women athletes as "invaders" and not meeting idealized standards of femininity. This has created unrealistic beauty standards for women in the media and barriers to women in positions of power and leadership. While cheerleading can be a demanding and challenging sport in a competitive context, in this case scenario it reflects the objectification of women for entertainment and sexist stereotypes in the sport workplace. It recognizes and accepts women only for their sex appeal and in roles that are designed to entertain and support men. The lack of fair compensation and disparate treatment based on sex trivializes the work, skills, and value of women to the organization. These attitudes and employment practices have led to a toxic culture problem in many sport organizations.

Ethical concepts that apply here include explicit bias and implicit bias. With explicit bias, a person is clear about their negative attitudes or behaviors toward others, and this might be evident in cases of intentional discrimination or harassment in the workplace. In contrast, implicit bias refers to bias that exists when persons unconsciously possess attitudes toward particular groups, or associate stereotypes with them. Implicit bias may lead to discriminatory practices as well, but sometimes the prejudice is outside a person's awareness or in apparent contradiction to their espoused beliefs and values. In this case scenario, the male-dominated league is acting on longstanding stereotypes about women and sexism by exploiting the women's squad in this way, through objectification, inequitable pay, and discriminatory work rules and conditions.

Case 2: *Sam is a high school athletic director (AD) at SKY High (SKY), a public high school located in a small, predominantly Christian community. Over the past 10 years, SKY won multiple state titles in football under the direction and leadership of Coach Tim (Tim), who is a devout Christian. Before and after each football game, Tim regularly leads his student-athletes and coaching staff in Christian prayer in the team locker room at SKY Stadium. Tim also individually kneels and recites a religious prayer on the 50-yard line for one minute at the conclusion of each game, after the teams shake hands. Tim wears his SKY-logoed coaching gear while praying at midfield. The local school district received an anonymous complaint about the prayers. They conducted interviews of all SKY football team members and determined that the majority of the team was Christian and that no one on the team raised any objections to the prayers. The school district and their legal counsel notified the AD and Tim that these forms of prayer are not permissible at a public school under applicable district policy. The AD belongs to the same church as Tim and did not want to offend him or lose a popular and successful coach. The AD privately told Tim that he did not have any problem with the prayers and he would not recommend any discipline if Tim continued the religious practices with his team, staff, and on the field.*

Case 2 is modeled on a "religious liberty" lawsuit filed by a former high school coach against his public school district, after he was fired for continuing to engage in religious prayers similar to those described in this case scenario. In *Kennedy v. Bremerton School District* (2021) the U.S. Supreme Court initially declined to hear an appeal filed by the former coach after a federal district court granted summary judgment in favor of the school district, dismissing the plaintiff's claims of discrimination based on religion under Title VII, and violation of his First Amendment right to free exercise of religion. In dismissing the case, the district court reaffirmed constitutional principles under the religion clauses of the First Amendment that are sometimes at odds—the free exercise clause and the establishment clause. The court noted that while public school employees have a First Amendment right to religious expression, the public school district has the right to enforce policies that restrict that expression if it violates prohibitions on the government endorsing or favoring a religion. As it relates to Title VII employment discrimination claims, the coach's violation of school policies in this regard was clearly a legitimate nondiscriminatory reason for his firing by the school district, and the termination was not based on the coach's religion. Thereafter, however, in January 2022, the U.S. Supreme Court granted certiorari on the First Amendment issues and conducted oral argument in April 2022. A decision has not yet been rendered at the time of this writing.

Ethically, in this hypothetical case scenario, the AD exhibited poor decision-making as he disregarded the law, district policy, and his superiors in order to keep and support his winning coach. Under these circumstances, the employment decisions by the AD should not have been influenced by the team's success or by the fact that the majority did not object to the coach's prayers. A "winning is everything" mentality led the AD to disregard school policy and constitutional requirements in a public school sport setting. The ethical concept of conformity bias also applies here, that is, the tendency to take cues for proper behavior by peer or social pressure, rather than independent judgment of what is right and wrong. In this case, despite clear direction from his superiors and legal counsel, the AD chose not to alienate or offend a successful and popular coach, or potentially upset the majority-Christian community of which he personally was a member.

Case 3: *For more than 30 years, noted sociologist Richard Lapchick, director of The Institute for Diversity and Ethics in Sport, has followed trends in racial and gender hiring in the four major professional sport leagues and college sports. He annually publishes a "Racial and Gender Report Card" for the NFL, NBA, MLB, NHL, and college sports, which is a comprehensive resource with data, analysis, and letter grades assigned to the respective areas. As of 2018, the average racial diversity of the workforce at the four major league headquarters was 33.3%, while gender diversity averaged 36.7%. At that time, the NBA was the leader in diversity hiring at the league office level, based on the Lapchick Reports, with rates of 36.4% and 39.6% for race and gender, respectively. (Lapchick, 2018). Over the last decade, changes in hiring priorities at sports organizations became evident with new executive roles created to oversee diversity and inclusion in the workplace.*

Case 3 is a scenario that presents best practices for employment by including diversity, equity, and inclusion. These are not necessarily legal obligations but rather sound ethical and business judgments. Corporate Social Responsibility, or CSR, refers to the need for businesses to be good corporate citizens. CSR involves going beyond the law's requirements in protecting the environment and contributing to social welfare. It is widely accepted as a moral and ethical obligation of modern business. A formal diversity, equity, and inclusion strategy is critical to an organization's overall corporate CSR program. CSR goes beyond earning money for shareholders. In the sport industry, it is concerned with protecting the interests of all stakeholders, including owners, coaches, athletes, and fans.

Certain sports, like hockey and lacrosse, are well-known for their lack of racial diversity. Many professional sport leagues have implemented new programs and initiatives devoted to inclusion and to attract a more diverse workforce that better reflects their fan base. Increasingly, women and minorities are being hired for management-level positions that were historically available only to White men. In NASCAR, for example, their program called Drive for Diversity was implemented to develop and draw minorities and women to the sport, primarily as drivers, but also including ownership, sponsorship, and crew member roles, designed to attract a more diverse audience to the sport. The stated philosophy of the NBA now includes a mission statement that diversity and inclusion are "central to the game" and "catalysts for innovation" (inclusion.nba.com). Other leagues have adopted similar mission statements and initiatives. In the NFL, the owners voluntarily adopted the Rooney Rule, to expand hiring opportunities for minorities in coaching and front office positions, by requiring teams to interview at least one minority candidate. These are not legal mandates or requirements, but good business decisions to promote an overall positive work culture that is welcoming, fair, and equitable.

Case 4: *Coach Sue is a female and head coach of women's lacrosse at BLUE University. Coach Bob is a male and head coach of men's lacrosse at the same school. The men's and women's teams have the same number of competitions and the same number of student-athletes on the respective rosters. Their teams practice the same number of hours at the same university facility. The teams have identical operating budgets and neither team generates revenue for BLUE. Bob was hired by BLUE in 2018. Sue was hired by BLUE in 2019. During the 2020–21 academic year, Coach Bob's salary was $50,000 higher than Coach Sue's salary. Neither coach had head coaching experience prior to being hired by BLUE. Last year, both teams were conference champions and ranked among the top ten teams in the country. After the conclusion of the 2020–21 season, BLUE gave each coach a $5,000 bonus and a 10% pay raise. The athletic director (AD) also changed Bob's job title from "Head Coach of Men's Lacrosse" to "Director of BLUE Lacrosse," without assigning Bob any additional responsibilities.*

Case 4 presents legal and ethical issues regarding fair pay for women in college coaching. In this scenario, the male and female head coaches are performing essentially the same job, as each position requires the same skill, effort, and responsibilities, under similar working conditions. In addition, the credentials and performance of the employees appear to be the same. However, the male head coach is paid $50,000 more than his female counterpart. Based on the stated facts, the only potential legal defense for BLUE to an Equal Pay Act or Title VII claim would be seniority inasmuch as Bob was hired one year before Sue. However, it is unlikely that an additional one year of seniority reasonably justifies the significant pay disparity favoring the male coach in this case.

In this scenario, BLUE and its AD are acting unethically by trying to circumvent the EPA and Title VII by arbitrarily giving Bob a new job title—"Director of BLUE Lacrosse"—which entailed no change in job responsibilities. The different title suggests that Bob received a promotion that justified his higher pay. Yet because Bob is still doing the same work as Sue, the new classification appears to be a mere pretext for unlawful discrimination based on sex. The AD tried to justify more pay for the male coach based on a new job title that is essentially a sham. Moreover, the director title alone projects an image to the BLUE community that the male's job is more prestigious than the woman's job, regardless of the salary. Historically, unethical employment practices like this were not uncommon in college athletic programs, and they continue in some programs to this day. In these cases, absent any legal justification, such as a legitimate seniority or merit system, administrators assume that male coaches should be paid more, regardless of actual responsibilities, credentials, and results. Such practices are based on outdated stereotypes and undervaluing the work of women employees, together with an underlying message about the trivialization of women's sports.

Closing Arguments

Sport managers must understand the fundamental legal principles of employment law and what constitutes illegal and unethical employment practices. Since the 1960s, civil rights laws have been enacted to provide important protections to employees against adverse employment actions and discrimination in the workplace. Legally, employers must understand and follow the law and implement employment policies and practices to ensure a nondiscriminatory work environment. These legal requirements are essential to the overall success of sport organizations and impact amateur, intercollegiate, and professional sport leagues, teams, athletes, and fans. To that same end, sport organizations should recognize their moral and ethical obligations to abide by principles of corporate social responsibility to create a more diverse and inclusive workforce, and ultimately, a healthy and positive work culture. Employers in the sport industry must seek to create meaningful change to its history of injustice that has marginalized underrepresented groups in sport management, coaching, and executive leadership.

Study Questions

1. What are the circumstances that could give rise to claims of wage discrimination based on sex under the Equal Pay Act in a college athletic program?
2. Describe different fact scenarios that present the elements of a claim of employment discrimination under Title VII of the Civil Rights Act of 1964. What are the available defenses for the employer?
3. Discuss the ethical decision-making issues faced by an institution after receiving internal complaints about sexual harassment by coaches.
4. What specific diversity and inclusive initiatives would you recommend for professional sport leagues? Describe the programs and employment measures that would best satisfy corporate social responsibility objectives.

Criminal Law: Sport Violence and Athlete Misconduct

CHAPTER 6

Opening Statement

There are two types of law under our U.S. justice system—civil law and criminal law. All the preceding chapters have addressed matters of civil law. Civil law is the body of law that relates to private rights or causes of action against others, usually seeking monetary damages as a remedy. In contrast, criminal law is the body of law that identifies criminal behavior and prescribes penalties for such conduct imposed by the state or federal government, including incarceration. Most criminal laws are enacted by state legislatures (state crimes) or U.S. Congress (federal crimes). Sport managers and athletes who engage in criminal conduct "off the field" may face prosecution by the state or federal government for violation of criminal statutes (e.g., driving while intoxicated, illegal gun possession, robbery, murder), and, if convicted, serve time in jail or prison, just as other citizens. This chapter focuses primarily on athlete violence "on the field" or "on the ice," raising questions that are unique to sport. That is, should our criminal laws be applied to athletes who engage in intentional and violent acts in a sport context, or should such matters be left to the discretion of sport governing bodies, including professional sport leagues, for imposition of appropriate discipline?

Section I of this chapter addresses the elements of criminal law, and crimes of assault and battery in particular. These crimes are examined because athletes who participate in inherently dangerous sports, like boxing, football, and hockey, frequently engage in violent conduct which would be subject to criminal charges for assault and battery if the same acts occurred in a non-sport setting. It explains that criminal matters involve prosecution by the state or federal government, not by private parties. The section also addresses why criminal cases are subject to a higher burden of proof than civil cases, and the rationale for criminal punishment (i.e., imprisonment). It looks closely at some "on the field" and "on the ice" examples of extreme athlete violence, the key factors that should be considered in evaluating criminal conduct, and the relative merits of league discipline versus governmental intervention in

LEARNING OBJECTIVES

After reading this chapter, students will:

1. Understand the differences between civil law and criminal law
2. Know the rationale for criminal punishment and the required burden of proof
3. Consider the ethical implications of conflicts of interest in league-imposed discipline in professional sports
4. Recognize the relative merits of league handling of discipline versus governmental intervention, such as laws, regulations, and criminal punishment
5. Understand the criminal and ethical aspects of doping in sport

professional sport violence. Finally, this section addresses some cases where athlete violence and criminality are motivated by a desire to gain a competitive advantage, by flaunting the rules of the game and harming an opponent in order to win.

Section II of this chapter addresses the ethical aspects of promoting good conduct in sport and punishing violent misconduct and rules violations with meaningful penalties beyond mere fines or suspensions. It examines conflicts of interest that have permeated sport leagues that purport to have responsibility for disciplining athletes but sometimes do so without transparency, or administer unfair, arbitrary, and/or overly lenient penalties that accomplish little to remedy the problem. Some sport organizations, including the NFL, have attempted to address these ethical concerns by implementing a personal conduct policy for acts that are criminal in nature or otherwise disparage the league brand. This includes proactive measures, such as education and prevention training for certain crimes, as well as victim resources and support. This section also examines criminal and ethical aspects of doping in sport, including state-sponsored doping, which cheats the system and often the athletes themselves. Other forms of cheating in sport are also examined in this context, which do not necessarily involve criminal conduct, but demonstrate that rule-breaking and violations of norms are often ignored and rationalized in a "winning is everything" sport environment.

I. The Law

Criminal Law: Fundamentals

Overview

Criminal law involves prosecution by the state or federal government for wrongful acts considered by society to be so egregious that they are a breach of peace. Crimes have long been identified and codified by state and federal lawmakers with prescribed punishments that may include incarceration. Crimes are considered offenses against the state, even if immediate harm is caused to an individual. This differs from civil law, which provides remedies via lawsuits for money damages or injunctions between parties, based on legal duties and responsibilities they owe to each other. In the United States, most crimes are prosecuted and punished at the state level, and most states have similar laws regarding criminal conduct such as murder, larceny, sexual assault, and so on, although penalties for those crimes may vary from state to state. Federal crimes include wrongful acts against the federal government, such as tax evasion or bank robbery, or interstate crimes like kidnapping and wire fraud. State crimes are prosecuted by local district attorneys or county prosecutors; federal crimes are prosecuted by U.S. attorneys based in each federal judicial district.

The legal terminology applicable to criminal and civil law is very different. In civil cases, terms such as "sued" and "liable" are used when someone commences a lawsuit and the other is found responsible. In criminal cases, charges are filed by the government, who in turn "prosecutes" a case against a criminal defendant, which may result in a verdict of "guilty" if the defendant is found criminally responsible. Importantly, the burden or standard of proof in a criminal case is higher than that in a civil case. The standard of proof in a civil case is known as a "preponderance of the evidence," meaning that a defendant may be liable for alleged acts if the case was proven more likely than not. However, the criminal standard of proof is much higher because a defendant's liberty is at stake, with potential incarceration if a guilty verdict is rendered. Criminal cases require that the prosecution prove their case "beyond a reasonable doubt." In criminal cases, a defendant is entitled to an attorney and a guilty jury verdict must be unanimous.

There are distinct rationales for the imposition of criminal punishment such as incarceration. One is the notion of rehabilitation; that is, that criminal sanctions will rehabilitate the offender, make them a more productive citizen, and prevent them from being a repeat offender. Another rationale is deterrence; that putting criminals in jail will deter others from committing similar offenses. An even broader rationale for criminal punishments has been based on an education theory, the idea that public awareness of criminal trials and sanctions will help educate the public on the law and the nature of what is right and wrong (Wong, 2010).

Many sports are inherently dangerous, involving violent physical contact that would constitute criminal assault and battery if it occurred off the field. However, with sport violence, the doctrine of consent is usually available to defend against criminal charges involving intentional physical acts that cause harm. Consent can be a valid defense to a crime if the victim knowingly and voluntarily gave it. For example, if an athlete is battered to the ground in a boxing match or a player is violently checked into the boards in a hockey game, criminal charges are inappropriate and unlikely because the victim voluntarily consented to participating in a dangerous sport involving physical fights. Yet there are many case examples of intentional and excessive violence between athletes that clearly occurred outside the rules of the game. In those cases, athletes are typically disciplined by their respective leagues or governing bodies, and criminal charges are still rare, for reasons explored further below.

Federal legislative efforts to control sport violence have been largely unsuccessful. For example, a proposed bill called the Sports Violence Act of 1980 attempted to regulate violence by amending the federal criminal code to establish a sentence of up to one year in prison and/or a $5,000 fine for professional athletes who knowingly use excessive physical force during games, causing risk of significant bodily injury to another person. That bill was not enacted into law. Subsequently, a federal bill known as the Sports Violence Arbitration Act of 1983 proposed to regulate professional sport leagues by mandating an arbitration system in each league to arbitrate grievances against players and their teams resulting from the use of excessively violent conduct. That legislation also failed to pass in Congress.

Criminal Assault and Battery

In the earlier chapter on tort law, we examined assault and battery in a civil law context. Both assault and battery are intentional torts, which means that a civil action for assault and/or battery may be filed between the parties to obtain monetary damages designed to compensate the victim for physical and emotional harm as well as economic losses. Both assault and battery are also crimes under state laws, and therefore subject to prosecution by the state. In cases of criminal assault or criminal battery, the punishment will vary depending on the law of the state where the offense was committed. Punishments may include imprisonment, depending on the severity of the offense and the criminal history of the perpetrator.

In the sections below, the crimes of assault and battery are defined. With each of these crimes, intent is a requirement. The main distinction between criminal assault and criminal battery is that contact is not necessary for an assault, while offensive contact must take place for battery. While assault and battery may be separate crimes, some states define assault and battery as one crime, which is committed when a person (a) tries to strike or physically does strike another, or (b) acts in a threatening manner to put another in fear of immediate harm. The following sets forth the requirements for conviction of assault and battery as separate crimes.

Assault

Criminal assault is typically defined as an intentional attempt or threat to injure or harm another person using violence or force. Although actual contact is not required, an assault requires an "act" that is overt or direct, that causes apprehension or fear to another for their safety. The second required element is intent; that is, that the offender intended the act that caused fear, even if they did not intend the specific harm.

Battery

The crime of battery involves intentional offensive or harmful touching of another person without their consent. It requires the following elements to prove a criminal case: (a) intent, (b) act, (c) physical contact, and (d) causation. In most jurisdictions, criminal battery is the considered to be the unlawful application of force to another that results in bodily injury.

Extreme Sport Violence—Case Examples

There are many case examples of extreme sport violence throughout sport history. These have occurred across a range of sports at all levels. In professional sports, high-profile athletes have engaged in egregious acts outside the rules of the game that in some cases have caused serious harm to others. These actions would undoubtedly constitute criminal conduct if they occurred in a non-sport setting. Yet these acts, when committed "on the field" or "on the ice," have rarely led to criminal charges, and it has been left to professional sport leagues to impose discipline. Some well-known violence examples in the four "major" professional sport leagues, with their respective legal implications, include the following.

Hockey

Professional hockey is well-known for violence on the ice. While the terms "enforcer" or "goon" are not included in the rules of hockey, most players and fans know what they mean, and fighting and vicious hits have always been a significant part of the game. Over the years, some have argued that the NHL actually promotes violence, as it is popular with spectators and brings attention to the sport. However, on some occasions, serious injury has resulted from intentional violent acts in hockey. Criminal investigations have ensued in some cases, as well as convictions for assault and assault with a weapon. It is rare that jail time is imposed; however, in 1988, NHL player Dino Ciccarelli hit an opposing player with a stick and was charged and convicted of assault, sentenced to one day in jail, and fined $1,000. It is within the discretion of the county prosecutor or district attorney whether or not to file criminal charges and, as discussed further below, many factors weigh into such decisions when violent acts causing bodily harm occur in the context of a professional sport.

Bertuzzi/Moore Incident

In 2004, a dispute between opposing players Todd Bertuzzi (Vancouver) and Steve Moore (Colorado) arose when Moore checked another Vancouver player, resulting in a concussion. No penalty was called on Moore and the league review determined it was a clean hit. Leading up to the next scheduled game between the teams, Bertuzzi made several statements suggesting he and his teammates would retaliate against Moore. While nothing occurred in that game, during the final regular season game between the two teams, Bertuzzi confronted Moore, trying to fight. Moore skated away and Bertuzzi followed Moore the length of the ice and back, finally sucker punching Moore from behind. Moore fell to the ice on his face while other players piled on, and Bertuzzi continued punching Moore. Moore was knocked unconscious and sustained three fractured vertebrae, a grade three concussion, vertebral ligament damage, stretching of brachial plexus nerves, and facial lacerations. Moore never played professional hockey again.

Moore filed a civil suit for monetary damages against Bertuzzi and the Vancouver Canucks. One of the legal issues in that case was assumption of risk based on the argument that hockey players knowingly and voluntarily participate in a dangerous game. Yet while rough play and fights are common in hockey, Moore's attorneys argued that Bertuzzi's actions were so outside the rules of the game that it was not an ordinary risk of hockey. Bertuzzi's conduct was planned and premeditated. Moore sought $68 million in damages and the case was eventually settled years later for an undisclosed amount. From a criminal standpoint, this was a rare case example of extreme sport violence that actually resulted in criminal charges. Bertuzzi was charged with assault by Canadian authorities and later given a conditional discharge after pleading guilty to the crime of assault causing bodily harm. He was ordered not to play in any sporting event in which Moore was participating and was also ordered to perform 80 hours of community service. The NHL suspended Bertuzzi for 20 games and fined the Vancouver Canucks the amount of $250,000. Bertuzzi was also banned from playing in any IIHF member league during the NHL lockout, for a period of 17 months, after which he was reinstated.

Simon/Hollweg Incident

In 2007, another hockey incident involving extreme violence occurred between players on rival teams, Chris Simon (NY Islanders) and Ryan Hollweg (NY Rangers). During the third period of the game, Hollweg checked Simon, who went face-first into the boards. There was no penalty assessed and play continued without interruption. In apparent retaliation, Simon struck Hollweg across his face and throat with his hockey stick. Simon was then ejected from the game. Although Simon's actions appeared excessively violent and dangerous, as it involved using his stick as a weapon to the head area, Hollweg was fortunate and not seriously injured, unlike Steve Moore in the preceding example. Hollweg suffered only a cut to the chin that required two stitches, likely because the strike from Simon's stick appeared to catch Hollweg's shoulder pads before hitting his face.

Simon was immediately suspended indefinitely by the NHL and then his suspension was set at 25 games, continuing into the next season. It was reported that the Nassau County district attorney considered filing criminal charges against Simon, however ultimately declined to do so. Some commentators noted that Simon's actions were not premeditated but occurred "in the heat of the moment," which would have mitigated, though not excused, culpability under criminal law. Interestingly, Simon's suspension at that time was one of the longest in NHL history. Yet, nine months later, Simon received a

30-game suspension for kicking an opponent with his skate blade. Obviously, the league discipline for the Hollweg incident did not deter or rehabilitate Simon, who was a repeat offender.

Football

Professional football is another inherently dangerous sport, as violent hits and tackles are part of the game. Injuries on the field are also commonplace, and civil suits between participants are rarely successful because of the doctrine of assumption of risk. However, on occasion, violent attacks have occurred when the ball was out of play and the actions were so outside the rules of the game that they have led to consideration of potential criminal charges. One such incident is described below.

Garrett/Rudolph Incident

In 2019, at the conclusion of a play, Myles Garrett (Cleveland Browns) ripped the helmet off the head of opposing quarterback Mason Rudolph (Pittsburgh Steelers), and began swinging at Rudolph with the helmet, landing at least one blow to the head. This led to a brawl, with several other players involved. Garrett received the longest suspension, which was initially called "indefinite" and then appealed. Garrett claimed that his attack was precipitated by Rudolph, who had uttered a racial slur towards him. The NFL investigation found that claim was unsubstantiated, and Garrett's suspension was set at six games. Another Steelers player, Maurkice Pouncey, received a three-game suspension for punching and kicking Garrett in the helmet in retaliation, and Browns payer Larry Ogunjobi received one game for pushing Rudolph to the ground on the side of the brawl.

To many observers, the use of a helmet as a weapon was shocking, even in the context of a dangerous game like football. It was reported that the Cleveland police stated that there were no charges filed against Garrett, and there was no police report filed by Rudolph or his team. Garrett's attack, however, could have been considered assault with a weapon, and a prosecutor might consider charges in future incidents of this nature. This was arguably an egregious and intentional act, so far outside the rules of the game that assumption of risk and consent would not be a viable defense to a civil action for monetary damages or criminal charges for assault with a weapon causing bodily harm, had Rudolph suffered serious injury.

Baseball

While baseball is not often considered among the most dangerous sports, Major League Baseball has a long history of violence in the form of bench-clearing brawls between teams. From May 2018 to May 2021, there were 17 bench-clearing incidents involving teams from NL Central division alone (Lacques, 2021). Most of those brawls resulted in MLB suspensions, depending on the facts and players involved. Generally, the brawls are precipitated by "dirty" plays, such as harmful slides, hit-by-pitches, or too-close inside pitches. Those underlying acts are often intentional but usually unpunished due to the "unwritten rules" of baseball, which turns a blind eye to this type of strategic violence. However, the brawls are clearly outside the rules of the game and involve fighting, assault, and battery while the game is not actually in play. Despite the physical injuries resulting from these brawls, there are no documented criminal cases from MLB history. In fact, in one of the most egregious acts of violence in the history of professional sports, a physical attack with a baseball bat over the head of an opposing player did not lead to criminal charges or any meaningful discipline from the league, as described below.

Marichal/Roseboro Incident

One of the most brutal acts of violence in sport occurred in Major League Baseball in 1965, during a game between rival teams, the Los Angeles Dodgers and San Francisco Giants. Early in the game, Giants pitcher Juan Marichal threw a high and inside pitch to a Dodgers player, knocking him down. When Marichal came to the plate to bat, the Dodgers catcher John Roseboro returned a ball to the mound, closely skimming past Marichal's face. Marichal confronted Roseboro, they exchanged words, and Marichal raised the bat and used it to strike Roseboro on the head. A bench-clearing brawl ensued and Marichal continued swinging the bat. Marichal was ejected and Roseboro left the game with a bleeding gash on his head that required 14 stitches.

The incident is especially well-known for the shocking leniency of the discipline imposed. Marichal was suspended for just eight game days and fined $1,750. A civil action was filed by Roseboro against Marichal, which was eventually settled for a reported $7,500. No criminal charges were brought by the local prosecutor in San Francisco, where the game was played, despite the intentionally violent act, the use of a baseball bat as a weapon, and the severity of the injuries to the victim.

Basketball

Basketball has seen numerous melees on the court, with penalties often assessed by the league for flagrant fouls during play. An incident involving physical violence between players and fans occurred in the NBA during the infamous "Malice at the Palace," when players from the Indiana Pacers climbed into the stands and engaged in physical fights with fans who had thrown items onto the court after a foul on a Pacers player. That notorious incident did lead to criminal charges filed against five players and seven fans involved, ranging from felony assault to trespassing. However, among all those charged, only one fan served any jail time, and nine players received league suspensions (Wong, 2010). However, in two other well-known acts of brutal violence in the NBA, one involving player versus player, and the other involving player versus coach, no criminal charges were filed against the perpetrators, and the players received what many consider overly lenient discipline by the league.

Washington/Tomjanovich Incident

In 1977, a vicious on-court attack occurred in an NBA game, when Kermit Washington of the LA Lakers deliberately swung and punched Houston Rockets player Rudy Tomjanovich in the face. Tomjanovich suffered severe injuries, including a fractured skull, broken jaw and nose, other facial injuries, and leakage of spinal fluid. Washington was fined $10,000 and suspended 60 days by the NBA. He resumed his career and became an all-star. No criminal charges were filed against Washington, but a jury awarded Tomjanovich $3.3 million in a civil action against the Lakers for failing to properly train and supervise their player, and keeping him on the team while aware of his propensity for violence. A civil lawsuit was also filed by the Rockets against the Lakers for the loss of Tomjanovich's services.

Sprewell/Carlesimo Incident

In 1997, a brutal assault by a player against his coach occurred during an NBA team practice. That incident arose when Golden State Warriors player Latrell Sprewell was angry after being criticized about his passes by Head Coach P. J. Carlesimo. Sprewell responded by threatening to kill Carlesimo, dragging him to the ground, and choking him for 10 to 15 seconds (Javier, 2000). Sprewell then left practice, returning 20 minutes later to attack Carlesimo again, throwing several punches and landing one. The next day, the Warriors suspended Sprewell without pay for 10 games. Following a massive public uproar about their handling of the incident, the Warriors reconsidered and voided Sprewell's contract. The NBA then suspended Sprewell for one year. No criminal charges were brought against Sprewell, notwithstanding the witnessed verbal threats and physical attacks.

A grievance arbitration was filed on behalf on Sprewell, and the arbitrator's decision was to reinstate Sprewell's contract with the Warriors and shorten the league suspension. While most observers might consider Sprewell's attacks premeditated, the arbitrator ruled differently, finding that the two separate assaults were "one transaction" and the result of anger and passion, not premeditation, which was a mitigating factor. The arbitrator ruled that the team and league penalties were therefore unreasonable and disproportionate. To many, this was another example of an athlete getting leniency for conduct that would be criminal in any other setting. Notably, a former NBA commissioner famously commented about the arbitrator's ruling, stating that "you cannot choke your boss and hold your job unless you play in the NBA" (Javier, 2000).

Violence to Gain a Competitive Advantage

The competitive nature and sometimes high stakes of sports have led to incidents of extreme violence motivated by the interests of the participant or fan in winning at all costs. These unfortunate incidents reflect premeditated criminal conduct to gain a competitive advantage in sport. Interestingly, two famous incidents in this regard occurred in women's sports, one perpetrated by a deranged fan, and the other an attack allegedly planned by a female competitor with apparent support of a group of sketchy associates.

The first of the women's incidents occurred in professional women's tennis in 1993, when a German man was allegedly upset that his favorite player, Steffi Graf, had been replaced as number one on the tour by 19-year-old Monica Seles. While Seles was playing a match against a different opponent, the fan walked down the aisle while Seles was seated on the changeover and stabbed her in the back with a 9-inch knife. Graf herself had no knowledge or involvement in the attack or any connection to the perpetrator. The physical and psychological harm to Seles was devastating, and she spent more than 2 years recovering before returning to the tour. The perpetrator received a 2-year suspended sentence in his native Germany and no jail time. The incident led to security enhancements on the part of the women's tour to protect players who were obviously vulnerable to danger while competing individually in unprotected match settings.

The other infamous attack in a women's sport was the assault on Nancy Kerrigan during the U.S. Figure Skating Championships in 1994. In that incident, which gained worldwide attention and notoriety, Kerrigan was struck by an unknown assailant with a baton across her leg when she left the ice after practice. Within days, a criminal plot was unraveled that involved persons close to Kerrigan's rival, Tonya Harding. It was suspected that Harding herself was somehow involved in the plans for the attack. The poorly executed plot was to knock Kerrigan out of the competition because it was the qualifier for the upcoming Olympic Winter Games in Lillehammer, Norway. Harming Kerrigan would pave the way for Harding to win. In fact, that part of the plan was successful, as Kerrigan was forced to withdraw due to the injury, and Harding won the title and was named to the U.S. Olympic Team. However, within a matter of days, three men, including Harding's ex-husband, were charged with criminal assault and conspiracy, and eventually served time in prison. Harding later admitted to covering up her knowledge of the attack after the fact, and the United States Olympic Committee initiated efforts to remove her from the team. However, those efforts were unsuccessful, and Harding did compete in Norway, finishing eighth overall. Following the Games, Harding pled guilty to conspiring to hinder prosecution, receiving 3 years' probation, 500 hours of community service, and a $160,000 fine. Her ultimate punishment came from the United States Figure Skating Association (USFSA), which was the national governing body for her sport. Following their investigation, Harding was forced to resign from the sport and forfeit her U.S. championship title.

An especially brazen, criminal-like plan to gain a competitive advantage in sport occurred in the NFL from 2009 to 2011, in a scandal known as "Bounty Gate." The scheme involved a bounty program under the direction of the New Orleans Saints defensive coordinator, paying team members bonuses to injure opposing players. The plot was eventually unraveled and included more than 20 Saints players, who received money with knowledge on the part of the coaching staff. These vicious attacks were motivated by both greed and the desire to win, and would constitute a criminal conspiracy and assault in any other context. However, the discipline was left solely to the league to administer and the criminal justice system did not intervene.

In 1997, a bizarre act of excessive violence outside the rules of sport occurred in the brutally violent sport of professional boxing. During the WBA Heavyweight Championship fight that year, Mike Tyson bit off part of the ear of his opponent, Evander Holyfield, and spit it out on the mat. This unprecedented intentionally violent and gruesome act was an effort by Tyson to gain a competitive advantage in the fight. Tyson was disqualified and fined $3 million by the Nevada Boxing Commission, but no criminal charges were filed in connection with the incident.

Finally, in a disturbing example of violence, ruthless competition, and the ethics of college sports, a back-up kicker for the University of Northern Colorado football team named Mitchell Cozad allegedly ambushed his teammate in a dimly lit parking lot and brutally stabbed him in the leg. Prosecutors argued that Cozad committed the crime because he was "obsessed with being the starting punter" and "the big man on campus." In 2007, Cozad was convicted of second-degree assault and sentenced to seven years in prison.

Punishment: League Handling Versus Governmental Intervention

As is clear from the above case examples, the problem of "on the field" violence in professional sports has been primarily the responsibility of leagues and team owners, as opposed to our criminal justice system. But as the severity and frequency of extreme sport violence increases, many observers are concerned that athlete discipline is far too lenient and that, in general, athletes receive special treatment for acts that would be considered criminal in any other context. The ability of leagues to implement meaningful penalties has been questioned as ineffective and arbitrary. Various forms of legislative action have been proposed as a potential solution to this problem, to define criminal acts in sport to ensure predictability and apply criminal sanctions (Wong, 2010).

Many recent examples of extreme violence in sports fit the elements of criminal assault and criminal battery. Such acts fall far enough outside the reasonable scope of risks associated with contact sports so as to render the consent defense inapplicable. Historically, our local prosecutors and criminal courts have taken a hands-off approach to such violence, and legislative attempts to define sport crimes and prescribe punishment have been unsuccessful. This has enabled major violent incidents to go relatively unpunished. As such, even a violent criminal conspiracy, like the Saints' bounty scandal, intended to cause harm to others for profit and team success, somehow avoided the purview of our criminal justice system.

There are various explanations for why sports and athletes have been insulated in this manner. First, our judges are not experts on the rules of the game and are not equipped to render quick and knowledgeable decisions on sport violence. Second, the culture of men's contact sports is one of toxic masculinity, where players are expected to be aggressive and violent, and fights between players are enjoyed and even celebrated by fans. Leagues are also in the position to promptly and efficiently review violent incidents and evaluate penalties based on specialized knowledge of the game.

However, leagues are not infallible in this regard, and sometimes apply inconsistent or overly lenient penalties due to conflicts of interest in protecting star players and the league brand. Also, athletes earning millions of dollars per year are typically not deterred by relatively small fines and short suspensions, as is evident by the many repeat offenders in various professional sport leagues. Moreover, from a public policy standpoint, it is important to ask whether a vicious attack intended to severely injure or maim another should be overlooked by society just because it happened on the field of play and not elsewhere (Ham, 2012). Many would argue that athletes should not be above the law simply because they participate in a contact sport. The adoption of laws that define and criminalize extreme sport violence could protect not only professional athletes, but athletes in college and high school as well. The laws would not apply to brutal body contact that is common and accepted in certain sports or consistent with the norms of the sport strategy, for example, collisions, hits, tackles, blocks, body checks, inside pitches, and so on, but would prohibit hit lists and bounties, and punish other types of intentionally malicious actions (Ham, 2012). Some possible standards to consider were identified in a Canadian case that sought to determine if valid consent to excessive violence existed in the context of an athletic event. Those factors were set forth in a five-part test: (a) nature of the game, (b) nature of the act, (c) the degree of force employed, (d) the degree of risk of injury, and (e) the state of mind of the accused (*Regina v. Cey*, 1989). Consideration of factors such as these would assist prosecutors and criminal courts in determining whether the conduct in question was incidental to the game and/or in the heat of the moment, as opposed to premeditated and intentional acts of excessive use of force and violence deserving of governmental intervention.

Off the Field Criminal Conduct

With regard to off the field criminal activity, athletes are subject to criminal charges and prosecution just like anyone else. Many athletes across a wide range of sports have been linked to crimes such as assault, illegal gun possession, sexual assault, and even murder. Professional sport leagues and teams have had to deal with these issues because they often receive widespread media attention and reflect poorly on the league itself. In 2006, the NFL hired a new commissioner, Roger Goodell, who faced immediate concerns about the league's image in light of dozens of criminal arrests of players, including recent arrests of nine players from the Cincinnati Bengals team alone. Goodell and the NFL Players Association agreed upon a personal conduct policy that would subject players to discipline for conduct that was "detrimental to the integrity of and public confidence in" the NFL. The policy defined prohibited conduct and provided for discipline as determined by the commissioner, including fines and suspensions. The implementation of the policy was criticized in some instances as arbitrary and unfair.

There was considerable controversy, for example, over lenient and inconsistent penalties for domestic violence offenses, which gained much attention in 2014 when a grand jury indicted NFL player Ray Rice on third-degree aggravated assault of his then-fiancée, which was evidenced on a video that went viral. The NFL imposed a two-game suspension on Rice under the policy. Following tremendous public outrage, the NFL revised their personal conduct policy in 2014 to more clearly define prohibited conduct to include domestic violence, and to lengthen bans to six games for a first domestic violence offense and a lifetime ban for a second incident. Page 1 of the NFL Personal Conduct Policy, as revised in 2018, is shown below, which applies to all league personnel as well as players. At page 1, the breadth and purpose of the updated policy is emphasized, and states that "conduct by anyone in the league that is illegal, violent, dangerous, or irresponsible puts innocent victims at risk, damages the reputation of others in the game, and undercuts public respect and support for the NFL" (NFL Personal Conduct Policy, 2018).

PERSONAL CONDUCT POLICY
League Policies for Players
2018

It is a privilege to be part of the National Football League. **Everyone** who is part of the league must refrain from "conduct detrimental to the integrity of and public confidence in" the NFL. This includes owners, coaches, players, other team employees, game officials, and employees of the league office, NFL Films, NFL Network, or any other NFL business.

Conduct by anyone in the league that is illegal, violent, dangerous, or irresponsible puts innocent victims at risk, damages the reputation of others in the game, and undercuts public respect and support for the NFL. We must endeavor at all times to be people of high character; we must show respect for others inside and outside our workplace; and we must strive to conduct ourselves in ways that favorably reflect on ourselves, our teams, the communities we represent, and the NFL.

To this end, the league has increased education regarding respect and appropriate behavior, has provided resources for all employees to assist them in conforming their behavior to the standards expected of them, and has made clear that the league's goal is to prevent violations of the Personal Conduct Policy. In order to uphold our high standards, when violations of this Personal Conduct Policy do occur, appropriate disciplinary action must follow.

This Personal Conduct Policy is issued pursuant to the Commissioner's authority under the Constitution and Bylaws, Collective Bargaining Agreement and NFL Player Contract to address and sanction conduct detrimental to the league and professional football. It applies to players under contract; all rookie players selected in the NFL college draft and all undrafted rookie players, unsigned veterans who were under contract in the prior League Year; and other prospective players once they commence negotiations with a club concerning employment.

Source: https://nflcommunications.com/Documents/2018%20Policies/2018%20Personal%20Conduct%20Policy.pdf

Setting a Precedent[1]

- *Regina v. Todd Bertuzzi*
- *Regina v. McSorley*
- *Regina v. Cey*
- *Regina v. Ciccarelli*

II. The Ethics

Case Scenarios

Case 1: *In 2019, authorities in Florida announced that NFL Patriots owner Robert Kraft was one of dozens of people whose names were linked to an alleged prostitution and human-trafficking sting. Kraft faced two misdemeanor solicitation charges for receiving sexual services while at a spa in Florida, where prostitution is illegal. Nearly a year and half later, charges against Kraft were dropped following a judge's ruling that video evidence of the services were not admissible at trial. Although the NFL Personal Conduct Policy on its face applies to anyone affiliated with the NFL, Kraft did not receive discipline under the policy.*

Case 1 presents legal issues as well as ethical issues with respect to alleged criminal activity by team owners in the NFL. Although players are usually the ones suspended, the policy language is clear that it applies more broadly. The first paragraph reads, "It is a privilege to be part of the National Football League. **Everyone** who is part of the league must refrain from 'conduct detrimental to the integrity of and public confidence in' the NFL. This includes owners, coaches, players, other team employees, game officials, and employees of the league office, NFL Films, NFL Network, or any other NFL business" (NFL Personal Conduct Policy, 2018; emphasis in original). In 2014, the NFL suspended Colts owner Jim Irsay for six games and fined him $500,000 for driving while impaired. Irsay is the only owner to be suspended by the league since 1999, when 49ers owner Eddie DeBartolo was suspended for the entire season for his part in a Louisiana gambling scandal.

Legally, Kraft was not convicted of a crime; however, that is not required for discipline under the policy. In fact, in the dismissal of the criminal proceedings, Kraft was not factually cleared of committing the underlying act of soliciting prostitution. Clearly, given the widespread media coverage of the incident and a public apology of sorts by Kraft himself, one could ethically conclude that Kraft's involvement in the incident was detrimental to the integrity of and public confidence in the NFL. Yet while players undoubtedly would have faced punishment, a wealthy, successful team owner like Kraft was unlikely to be suspended by the commissioner he employs. Unsurprisingly, the NFL did not issue

---

1 The listed cases involved criminal charges under Canadian law. Each case arose from athlete violence in professional hockey.

discipline under the policy, as the Patriots were about to commemorate their sixth Super Bowl title under Kraft's ownership.

It is ethically problematic that the NFL Personal Conduct Policy is subject to selective enforcement by the commissioner. While the policy purports to apply to all, there are clear conflicts of interest when wealthy and powerful team owners engage in misconduct that arguably diminishes the integrity of the league. As the chief executive officer of the league, the commissioner is hired by the team owners. He also plays a substantial role as decision-maker in imposing discipline under the policy. It seems likely that a player accused of a similarly salacious crime, one that is widely publicized with video evidence, would be thoroughly investigated and disciplined by the league under the policy, regardless of a criminal conviction. The Kraft case highlights inequities and ethical lapses in turning a blind eye to prohibited conduct committed by a powerful and successful team owner.

Case 2: *Toward the end of her successful professional tennis career, Maria Sharapova was implicated in a drug scandal that resulted in her suspension from the women's tour. At the 2016 Australian Open, Sharapova tested positive for meldonium, a drug usually prescribed for heart conditions, that had recently been added to the World Anti-Doping Agency (WADA) banned list of substances. Sharapova initially described this as an oversight on her part, and that she had overlooked notice of the drug being added to the list. Meldonium is legal to use in Russia, which was the country Sharapova represented. She claimed to have been taking the medicine for 10 years for health issues. Meldonium was very popular among athletes and was used by the Soviet military for optimizing the use of oxygen. As a result of the positive drug test, Sharapova was suspended for 2 years by the International Tennis Federation (ITF). On appeal to the Court of Arbitration for Sport (CAS), the panel reduced the suspension to 15 months. A few of Sharapova's many sponsors suspended their relationships with her. Some resumed the relationship after she returned to compete on the tour. Sharapova retired from the sport in 2020.*

Case 2 involves alleged doping by high-profile professional athlete that was not a crime but did violate the rules of the sport. If proven to be intentional, this type of cheating is both immoral and unethical. There are countless scandals in sport history of athletes using performance-enhancing drugs to gain a competitive edge and/or masking agents to conceal their use in drug testing by governing bodies. Although certain illegal drug use may be criminal, the performance-enhancing drugs in question in sport are frequently not illegal, but rather constitute cheating because the individual benefits by using prohibited substances in their sport competition. Doping has even impacted the sport of horse racing, as there was widespread speculation that the 2021 Kentucky Derby–winning horse was given prohibited corticosteroids by a trainer. The trainer was then banned by New York racing officials from running any of his horses at the subsequent Belmont Stakes.

Throughout her career, Sharapova was among the highest-paid female athletes in the world, based on her tour winnings and massive endorsement deals. Her explanation that she was unaware of the banned drug lacked credibility, given her huge team of agents and attorneys whose job it was to stay apprised of matters such as WADA rules. Also, while her suspension was eventually reduced by the CAS panel, many of Sharapova's competitors on the tour remained skeptical of her medical defense. It seemed transparently self-serving and implausible that a world-class tennis player had been treated with heart medication for 10 years beginning at a very young age, with no reported indicators of chronic illness, and that the medication happened to be popular among Russian athletes, with documented benefits such as increased endurance and improved recovery time after exercise. Interestingly, while a few corporate sponsors dropped her to avoid association with an alleged cheater, most set aside these ethical considerations, as Sharapova regained many of those endorsements and added more after returning to the tour. It seems that despite her alleged transgressions, Sharapova was still a highly popular and attractive athlete, and, taking everything into account, was still considered valuable to corporate interests and brands.

Athletes who cheat via doping typically try to deny or rationalize their conduct when caught. A common defense to positive drug tests for athletes is that they were administered the drug "inadvertently," expecting others to believe that someone slipped the drug into their drink or nutritional supplements without their knowledge. Another defense is blame shifting, asserting that the testing was in error, or that someone maliciously switched samples to falsely implicate them. These defenses are consistent with the ethical concept of self-serving bias, or the common habit of a person taking credit for positive events or outcomes but blaming outside factors for negative events. For example, some athletes will attribute winning games or events to their hard work and practice, yet blame their losses on unfair rules or bad calls by referees.

Another common defense to doping is the ethical rationalization that "everyone else is doing it" and that their illegal drug use is acceptable because it was only intended to "level the playing field." This type of rationalization was offered in the massive drug cheating associated with Lance Armstrong in cycling. When Armstrong finally "confessed" to years of systematic doping in his widely viewed television interview with Oprah Winfrey, he continued to deny that he was a cheater. His rationalization was that doping was so widespread in cycling that it was a "necessary evil" to enable him to compete on a level playing field. This is nothing more than a variation on the ethical justification that bad acts are acceptable because others are doing the same thing.

Case 3: *You are a sport policy advisor briefing your country's representative at the International Olympic Committee (IOC) meeting prior to the Olympic Games. You have heard and seen compelling evidence of state-sponsored doping by Russia presented by the World Anti-Doping Agency (WADA) and an independent investigative report. There is strong evidence that many Russian athletes have doped and that the cheating was orchestrated by the Russian sport ministry, anti-doping labs, and intelligence services. The Russian government firmly denies any state program, and that if doping happened, it was isolated incidents by rogue elements. Russia further claims that the accusations are attempts by its enemies to discredit its athletes, who have trained hard and competed fairly. The credibility of the Olympic movement is at stake, but you are also conscious of not wanting to politicize the Games or punish those who have done no wrong. While the evidence of some cheating is strong, you are not a scientist, and there are many Russian athletes who are likely to be clean. The committee will be voting on several options regarding Russian participation. How would you best advise your country's representative on the ethical and policy implications of the handling of this matter?*

Case 3 is modeled on a state-sponsored doping scandal that allegedly transpired over a number of years in Russia. This type of scandal is different from individual cases such as Armstrong or Sharapova because the banned drugs were allegedly supplied to athletes by the state. State-sponsored doping was prevalent for decades in the communist government of the former German Democratic Republic (GDR or East Germany) as part of a geopolitical strategy. Olympic medals and success at the Games were a means to bolster the state image and increase political power. The East German doping system started in the 1960s and was formalized through the government sport ministry and kept top secret. Through systematic doping of young athletes, without their knowledge, East Germany amassed many medals and competitive success while causing severe physical and mental harm to their individual athletes. The system ended in the 1990s with the fall of the Berlin Wall. In the aftermath, criminal sanctions were imposed on some doctors and coaches for administering illegal drugs to minors, and many former athletes who unwittingly took the drugs received financial compensation for the adverse effects they suffered.

Dozens of Russian athletes who competed at the 2014 Sochi Olympic Games, including at least 15 medal winners, were found to be part of a Russian state-run doping program. This discovery was based on evidence of widespread doping violations among Russian athletes, including efforts to manipulate data and sabotage doping investigations. As a result, in 2019, WADA banned Russia from all major sporting events for 4 years. In 2020, upon an appeal by Russia, the CAS reduced the ban to 2 years, through December 2022. Under the ruling, individual competitors from Russia were allowed to compete in international competitions under a neutral flag and designation. The CAS panel wrote that the punishments imposed were not as extensive as those sought by WADA, but that this was not a "validation" of the conduct of the Russian Anti-Doping Agency (RUSADA) or the Russian authorities.

In February 2022, during the Beijing Olympic Games, another Russian doping controversy arose involving medal-favorite Russian skater Kamila Valieva, age 15, who tested positive for trimetazidine, a banned heart medication considered to be a performance-enhancing drug. Due to the earlier state-imposed ban, Valieva was representing the "ROC" (Russian Olympic Committee) under a neutral flag. In a controversial ruling by the CAS, Valieva was cleared to compete in Beijing despite her positive test.

Case 4: *In 2017, the Houston Astros won the World Series. Two years later, a former Astros player publicly disclosed that the Astros had participated in a major sign-stealing scheme during their championship year. MLB launched an investigation that granted the Astros players immunity in return for specific information. It was revealed that, throughout the 2017 season, the team was stealing signs by using a camera in center field to record the opposing team's catcher's signs to the pitcher, and then relaying it in real time to the Houston batter by banging on a trash can. Ultimately, MLB Commissioner Rob Manfred imposed discipline on many of those involved in the sign-stealing scheme. In January 2020, the commissioner's report and decision found that most of the Astros' players knew of the scheme and many participated in it. The report said that manager Hinch knew of the scheme, and that GM Luhnow should have prevented it. Commissioner Manfred suspended both Hinch and Luhnow, who were quickly fired by Astros owner Crane. MLB fined the Astros $5 million, and stripped the club of its first- and second-round draft picks in both 2020 and 2021. The commissioner's decision did not include any discipline for individual players, and the Astros retained their 2017 World Series title (Statement of Commissioner, 2020).*

Case 4 presents legal and ethical issues that relate to cheating in a major professional sport. The history of baseball is filled with cheating scandals going back to 1919, with allegations over the years including deliberately throwing games in coordination with gamblers, use of spit balls and corked bats, and the widespread use of performance-enhancing drugs. Some of the underlying cheating and misconduct was criminal in nature, such as illegal gambling and illegal drug use. Other bad acts were "illegal" in the sense that they violated MLB rules and norms. The Astros scandal is noteworthy because the team knowingly crossed the ethical line of "regular" sign-stealing, which is accepted as part of the game, to technology-aided or electronic sign-stealing, which was prohibited under the MLB rules and threatened the integrity of the game.

From a legal standpoint, the Astros scandal did not result in any physical harm or criminal charges. However, their scheme violated MLB regulations, which prohibit the use of electronic equipment during games, and state that no such equipment "may be used for the purpose of stealing signs or conveying information designed to give a Club an advantage" (Statement of Commissioner, 2020). It also led to several civil lawsuits against the Astros' organization and MLB, brought by fans, ticketholders, online sport gamblers, and at least one opposing player. Those civil cases were based on various legal theories that the games were knowingly rigged and constituted deceptive consumer trade practices and civil fraud. The opposing player was a pitcher who had poor results in his outings against the Astros. His suit alleged that the Astros engaged in unfair business practices, negligence, and intentional interference with contractual and economic relations, causing him substantial economic losses, as he was demoted to the minor leagues after those games.

The knowing participation of so many athletes in this scheme is of course ethically problematic. It is perhaps explained that they felt compelled to go along with it out of obedience to authority and did not speak out because they followed a "code of silence" to protect the team. Another explanation is incrementalism, or the slippery slope that occurs when ethically questionable actions increase from ordinary sign-stealing or dirty plays to more serious offenses, when the result is winning and individual success. Over time, the players lowered their ethical standards by continuing to engage in the scheme throughout the long season without any consequences. Yet, they knowingly and self-servingly received the benefits of improved performance on the field. Further, the active role of the team manager and owners reflects ethical decision-making motivated by profit and winning at all costs. MLB is among the major competitive environments in all of sport, with hundreds of millions of dollars, corporate brands, and tremendous prestige at stake for organizations competing for World Series titles. Many players, managers, owners, and fans will set aside ethics in order to win.

The commissioner's decision not to discipline players was widely criticized. He asserted that granting immunity in exchange for information was the best way to obtain the truth (Prentice, 2020). Unfortunately, the scandal will leave lasting damage to the MLB, the Astros' organization, the individual players involved, and the integrity of the game of baseball.

Closing Arguments

Sport managers, leagues, athletes, and fans should recognize the elements of criminal law and how those elements can apply to intentional acts of violence in inherently dangerous sports. They should consider the purposes of criminal punishment in our legal system and whether athletes should be subject to charges for extreme violent acts that would be criminal if they occurred in a non-sport setting. Governmental intervention might be appropriate in cases of premeditated acts of extreme sport violence. The motivations for athlete violence and criminality are also important to understand, as sports sometimes encounter excessive violence due to a desire to gain a competitive advantage. This involves teams and athletes deliberately flaunting the rules of the game or intentionally harming an opponent in order to win. Sport managers should engage in ethical decision-making that promotes good conduct on and off the field and imposes meaningful punishment for violent misconduct and flagrant rules violations. This requires the implementation of disciplinary policies that are not arbitrary or selectively enforced. Finally, sport organizations should be vigilant in adhering to ethical standards to reduce cheating in sport because it is increasingly widespread and harmful when not called out and severely punished. Discipline must be both firm and consistent to support the values of maintaining a safe playing environment, fair competition, and the overall integrity of the game.

Study Questions

1. What are the pros and cons of league handling versus governmental intervention with respect to acts of extreme violence by athletes? What aspects of criminal law are relevant to this analysis?
2. Do you think that the NFL Personal Conduct Policy is fair in allowing the imposition of discipline for acts that do not involve formal criminal charges or convictions?
3. Discuss the ethical decision-making issues faced by teams and leagues when a star player tests positive for performance-enhancing drugs.
4. Read the findings of the MLB commissioner with regard to the Houston Astros' sign-stealing scandal. Do you agree with the discipline that was imposed? Why/why not?
5. What are the ethical implications involving minor athletes from countries involved in state-sponsored doping programs?

References

Chapter One

Fine, T. M. (1997). *American legal systems: A resource and reference guide.* Anderson Pub. Co.

Hanson, K. & Savage, M. (2012). What role does ethics play in sports? *Santa Clara University Institute for Sports Law and Ethics.* https://www.scu.edu/ethics/focus-areas/more-focus-areas/resources/sports-ethics-mapping-the-issues/

Reginald Bush v. St. Louis Reg'l Convention and Sports Complex Authority, No. 1622-CC00013, 2016 WL 11295572 (Mo. Cir. Ct. Jan. 15, 2016).

Chapter Two

ESPN News Services. (2018, June 12). Jury orders Rams to pay Reggie Bush $12.5M for 2015 injury. *ESPN.* https://www.espn.com/nfl/story/_/id/23773883/los-angeles-rams-ordered-pay-reggie-bush-125m-injury

Bearman v. University of Notre Dame, 453 N.E.2d 1196 (Ind. App. 1983).

Benejam v. Detroit Tigers, Inc., 635 N.W.2d 219 (Mich. App. 2001).

Bourne v. Gilman, 452 F.3d. 632 (7th Cir. 2006).

Chayes, M. (2021, March 3). Mom of Sachem High teen killed in football training mishap settles suit. *Newsday.* https://www.newsday.com/long-island/suffolk/sachem-high-school-joshua-mileto-lawsuit-o51795

Champion, W. T. (2001). *Sports law in a nutshell.* West Group.

DeMauro v. Tusculum College, Inc., 603 S.W.2d 115 (Tenn. 1980).

Eddy v. Syracuse University, 78 A.D.2d 989 (N.Y. App. Div. 1980).

Filler v. Rayex Corporation, 435 F.2d 336 (7th Cir. 1970).

Graham, B. A. (2019, October 2). Former UC Berkeley cheerleader says coaches ignored concussions in lawsuit. *The Guardian.* https://www.theguardian.com/sport/2019/oct/02/cal-cheerleader-concussion-lawsuit-melissa-martin

Hackbart v. Cincinnati Bengals, Inc., 601 F.2d 516 (10th Cir. 1979).

Keeton, W. P. (1984). *Prosser and Keeton on torts* (5th ed.). West Group.

Kleinknecht v. Gettysburg College, 989 F.2d 1360 (3d. Cir. 1993).

Moore v. Bertuzzi, Ont. Super. Ct. 2006.

Nabozny v. Barnhill, 334 N.E.2d 258 (Ill. App. 1975).

Otero-Amad, F. (2019). Former U.C. Berkeley cheerleader sues coaches and school for ignoring repeated concussions. https://nbcnews.com/news/sports/former-u-c-berkeley-cheerleader-sues-coaches-school-ignoring-repeated-n1062696

Restatement (Second) of Torts §§ 282, 432 (Am. L. Inst. 1965).

Spengler, J. O., Anderson, P. M., Connaughton, D., & Baker, T. A. (2016). *Introduction to sport law*. Human Kinetics.

Stringer v. Minnesota Vikings Football Club, LLC, 705 N.W.2d 746 (Minn. 2005).

University of Notre Dame. (2011). *Investigation report October 27, 2010 aerial lift accident*. https://nd.edu/assets/docs/notr-dame-investigation-report.pdf

VerdictSearch. (2018). *Student: School failed to follow concussion protocol*. https://verdictsearch.com/verdict/student-school-failed-to-follow-concussion-protocol/#

Walters Inc. (2018). *An independent evaluation of procedures and protocols related to the June 2018 death of a University of Maryland football student-athlete*. https://usmd.edu/newsroom/Walters-Report-to-USM-Board-of-Regents.pdf

Chapter Three

15 U.S.C. §§ 7801–7807.

Baird, N. (2020, June 16). What Ohio State's 'Buckeye Pledge' COVID-19 risk acknowledgment really says, and why legal experts take issue. *Cleveland.com*. https://www.cleveland.com/osu/2020/06/what-ohio-states-buckeye-pledge-covid-19-risk-acknowledgment-really-says-and-why-legal-experts-take-issue.html

Beaty v. Kansas Athletics, Inc., Case No. 19-2137-KHV-GEB (D. Kan. 2019).

Levert v. University of Illinois at Urbana/Champaign through the Board of Trustees, No. 2002 CA 2679, 2002 CA 2680 (La. Ct. App. 2003).

National Basketball Players Association. (2017, January 19). *Collective bargaining agreement (CBA)*. https://nbpa.com/cba

National Letter of Intent. (n.d.). *NLI frequently asked questions*. http://www.nationalletter.org/frequentlyAsked-Questions/index.html

NCAA Bylaw 15.3.3.1, as amended. National Collegiate Athletic Association. (2020). *2020–2021 NCAA Division I manual*. https://www.ncaapublications.com

Norlander, M. (2015, June 4). UNC scandal: Allegations, responses and a timeline on what's to come. *CBS Sports*. https://www.cbssports.com/college-basketball/news/unc-scandal-allegations-responses-and-a-timeline-on-whats-to-come

N.C. Gen. Stat. §§ 78C-85–78C-105 (2014).

Restatement (Second) of Contracts §§ 2, 24 (Am. L. Inst. 1990).

Rodgers v. Georgia Tech Athletic Association, 303 S.E.2d 467 (Ga. Ct. App. 1983).

Smith, J. M., & Willingham, M. (2015). *Cheated: The UNC scandal, the education of athletes, and the future of big-time college sports*. Potomac Books.

Taylor v. Wake Forest University, 191 S.E.2d 379 (N.C. App. 1972).

Tracy, M. (2017, October 13). N.C.A.A.: North Carolina will not be punished for academic scandal. *The New York Times.* https://www.nytimes.com/2017/10/13/sports/unc-north-carolina-ncaa.html

Vanderbilt University v. DiNardo, 174 F.3d 751 (6th Cir. 1999).

Wainstein, K., Jay, A. J., & Depman Kukowski, C. (2014, October 16). *Investigation of irregular classes in the Department of African and Afro-American Studies at the University of North Carolina at Chapel Hill.* Cadwalader.

Williamson v. Prime Sports Marketing, LLC, 1:19-cv-593 (M.D.N.C. 2019).

Witz, B. (2020, June 17). Welcome back to football (terms and conditions apply). *The New York Times.* https://www.nytimes.com/2020/06/17/sports/ncaafootball/coronavirus-college-football-waivers.html

Chapter Four

20 U.S.C. §§ 1681–1688.

34 C.F.R. § 106.37(c)(1).

42 U.S.C. § 2000d *et. seq.*

AIAW v. NCAA, 735 F.2d 577 (D.C. Cir. 1984).

Biediger v. Quinnipiac University, 691 F. 3d 85 (2012).

Boucher v. Syracuse University, 164 F.3d 113 (2d Cir. 1999).

Cannon v. University of Chicago, 441 U.S. 677 (1979).

Cohen v. Brown University, 101 F.3d 155 (1st Cir. 1996).

Empowering Olympic, Paralympic, and Amateur Athletes Act of 2020, Pub. Law No. 116-189 (10/30/2020).

Franklin v. Gwinnett County Public Schools, 503 U.S. 60 (1992).

Gebser v. Lago Vista Independent School District, 524 U.S. 274 (1998).

Grove City College v. Bell, 465 U.S. 555 (1984).

Jackson v. Birmingham Board of Education, 544 U.S. 167 (2005).

Kliegman, J. (2020, June 30). Idaho banned trans athletes from women's sports. She's fighting back." *Sports Illustrated.* https://www.si.com/sports-illustrated/2020/06/30/idaho-transgender-ban-fighting-back

National Collegiate Athletic Association v. Joseph Califano, 444 F. Supp. 425 (D. Kan. 1978).

NCAA Office of Inclusion. (2011, August). *NCAA Inclusion of Transgender Student-Athletes.* https://www.ncaaorg.s3.amazonaws.com/inclusion/lgbtq/INC_TransgenderHandbook.pdf

National Women's Law Center. (2017, June). *Debunking the myths about Title IX and athletics.* https://nwlc.org/wp-content/uploads/2015/08/Title-IX-Athletics-Myths.pdf

National Wrestling Coaches Association v. U.S. Department of Education, 263 F. Supp. 2d 82 (D. D.C. 2003).

Office for Civil Rights. (1998, July 23). *Dear Colleague Letter: Bowling Green State University.* U.S. Department of Education.

Office for Civil Rights. (2016, May 13). *Dear Colleague Letter: Transgender Students.* U.S. Department of Education.

Richards v. USTA, 93 Misc. 2d 713 (N.Y. Sup. Ct. 1977).

Riley, L. (2021) Federal judge dismisses lawsuit that sought to block transgender female athletes from competing in girls high school sports in Connecticut. *Hartford Courant.* https:www.courant.com/sports/high-schools/hc-sp-hs-transgender-case-dismissal-20210425-twgpmkmsrvhnhl64u2tr32tg3y-story.html

Safe Sport Authorization Act of 2017, 36 U.S.C. § 220541.

Thomas, K. (2011, July 28). Gender games: Long fights for sports equity, even with a law. *The New York Times.* https:www.nytimes.com/2011/07/29/sports/review-shows-title-ix-is-not-significantly-enforced.html

Women's Sports Foundation. (2020, January). *Chasing equity: The triumphs, challenges, and opportunities in sports for girls and women.* https://www.womenssportsfoundation.org/wp-content/uploads/2020/01/Chasing-Equity-Executive-Summary.pdf

Chapter Five

29 U.S.C. § 206(d).
29 C.F.R. § 1604.11(a)(1).
29 C.F.R. § 1604.11(e).
29 U.S.C. § 157.
29 U.S.C. §§ 621 *et seq.*
42 U.S.C. §§ 12101 *et seq.*
42 U.S.C § 2000e-2(a).

Anderson, G. (2020, June 16). 'Far-Reaching Consequences': U.S. Supreme Court's landmark ruling extending protections against employment discrimination to LGBTQ people has implications for how colleges define sex and enforce gender equality on campus. *Inside Higher Ed.* https://www.insidehighered.com/news/2020/06/16/landmark-supreme-court-ruling-could-redefine-title-ix

Bostock v. Clayton County, Georgia, 590 U.S. ___, 140 S. Ct. 1731 (2020).

Coleman v. Western Michigan University, 336 N.W.2d 224 (Mich. App. 1983).

Das, A. (2022). U.S. soccer and women's players agree to settle equal pay lawsuit. *The New York Times.* https//www.newyorktimes.com/2022/02/22/sports/soccer/us-womens-soccer-equal-pay.html

Dawson v. National Collegiate Athletic Association, 250 F. Supp. 3d 401 (N.D. Cal. 2017) (aff'd, 9th Cir. 2019).

NBA. (n.d.). *NBA diversity and inclusion.* https://www.inclusion.nba.com

Kennedy, J. F. (1963, June 19). *Special message to the Congress on civil rights and job opportunities.* The American Presidency Project. https://www.presidency.ucsb.edu/documents/special-message-the-congress-civil-rights-and-job-opportunities

Lapchick, R. (2018). *The 2018 racial and gender report card: National Basketball Association.* Institute for Diversity and Ethics in Sport.

Ledbetter v. Goodyear Tire & Rubber Company, 550 U.S. 618 (2007).

Lombardo, J., & Mullen, L. (2018). Gaining momentum. Street & Smith's Sports Business Journal. https://www.sportsbusinessjournal.com/Journal/Issues/2018/7/30/In-Depth/Main.aspx

Medcalf v. Trustees of the University of Pennsylvania, 71 F. App'x 924 (3d Cir. 2003).

Moore v. University of Notre Dame, 22 F. Supp. 2d 896 (N.D. Ind. 1998).

Morgan v. United States Soccer Federation, Inc., 445 F. Supp. 3d 635 (C.D. Cal. 2020).

Northwestern University and College Athletes Players Association (CAPA), Case 13-RC-121359 (NLRB Region 13, 2014).

Ortiz-Del Valle v. National Basketball Association, 42 F. Supp. 2d 334 (S.D.N.Y. 1999).

Perdue v. City Univ. of New York, 13 F. Supp. 2d 326 (E.D.N.Y. 1998).

PGA Tour, Inc. v. Martin, 532 U.S. 661 (2001).

Rensing v. Indiana State University Board of Trustees, 437 N.E.2d 78 (Ind. Ct. App. 1982).

Stanley v. University of Southern California, 178 F.3d 1069 (9th Cir. 1999).

U.S. Equal Employment Opportunity Commission. (2020, January 24). *EEOC releases fiscal year 2019 enforcement and litigation data.* https://www.eeoc.gov/newsroom/eeoc-releases-fiscal-year-2019-enforcement-and-litigation-data

Chapter Six

Justia. (n.d.). *Assault and battery.* https://www.justia.com/criminal/offenses/violent-crimes/assault-battery

NFL. (2018). *Personal conduct policy: League policies for players 2018.* https://nflcommunications.com/Documents/2018%20Policies/2018%20Personal%20Conduct%20Policy.pdf

USLegal. (n.d.). *Sports violence.* https://sportslaw.uslegal.com/sports-violence

Brewer, J. (2019, July 30). The NFL's Roger Goodell doesn't care about integrity or consistency. The Robert Kraft case proves it. *The Washington Post.* https://www.washingtonpost.com/sports/nfl/roger-goodell-doesnt-care-about-integrity-or-consistency-the-robert-kraft-case-proves-it/2019/07/29/beb739dc-b230-11e9-8f6c-7828e68cb15f_story.html

Graham, P. (2007, August 25). 'The heartache is unbearable': Family carries on after punter's conviction. *Casper Star Tribune.* https://trib.com/news/state-and-regional/the-heartache-is-unbearable-family-carries-on-after-punters-conviction/article_fda56c4e-57fa-5e60-a58b-b1859152237e.html

Ham, E. L. (2012, March 7). Give the ref a gavel. *The New York Times.* https://www.nytimes.com/2012/03/08/opinion/prosecute-excess-violence-in-sports.html

Javier, R. A. (2000). You cannot choke your boss & (and) hold your job unless you play in the NBA: The Latrell Sprewell incident undermines disciplinary authority in the NBA. *Jeffrey S. Moorad Sports Law Journal,* 7(2), 209. https://digitalcommons.law.villanova.edu/mslj/vol7/iss2/2/

Lacques, G. (2021, May 10). 'There is a lot of testosterone:' Why beefs and brawls are a way of life in the NL Central. *USA Today.* https://www.usatoday.com/in-depth/sports/mlb/2021/05/10/basebrawl-why-beefs-and-brawls-way-life-nl-central/4974822001/

Manfred, Jr., R. D. (2020, January 13). *Statement of the commissioner.* https://img.mlbstatic.com/mlb-images/image/upload/mlb/cglrhmlrwwbkacty27l7.pdf

Thornton, P. K. (2017). Rewriting hockey's unwritten rules: Moore v. Bertuzzi. *Maine Law Review, 61*(1), 205. https://digitalcommons.mainelaw.maine.edu/mlr/vol61/iss1/8

Wong, G. M. (2010). *Essentials of sports law* (4th ed.). Praeger Publishers.

About the Author

MARISSA W. POLLICK, JD

Marissa W. Pollick is an attorney and lecturer in sport management at the University of Michigan. She has more than three decades of experience as a litigator in employment law, civil rights, and commercial contracts. Since 2008, Marissa has also served as an expert consultant to schools and universities on Title IX compliance. She has taught undergraduate and graduate courses in sports law and ethics, sport and public policy, and race and cultural issues in sport. She is a graduate of the University of Michigan (BA, History, with High Distinction, 1978) and the University of Michigan Law School (JD, 1981).

As an undergraduate at Michigan, Marissa was a 4-year letter winner and two-time co-captain of the women's tennis team and was among the first women in Michigan history to be awarded a varsity "Block M" and athletic scholarship. As a lawyer and advocate, she was later instrumental in eliminating century-old gender restrictions on varsity club membership at Michigan and was elected the "M" Club's first woman President in 1999–2000.

Marissa was among the initial inductees in the University of Michigan M-Women Academic/Athletic Hall of Honor. In 2002, she was the first woman athlete inducted into the State of Michigan Jewish Sports Hall of Fame. She has lectured across the country on the topics of sex discrimination in sport, Title IX athletic compliance, and sexual harassment and assault under Title IX, and served as lead counsel in Title IX litigation on behalf of women athletes, coaches, and administrators.